Empower

Publishing

Watch for More Titles by Elie B. Mbumina

and Empower Publishing

My Incredible Story of My Coming to America—A Land of Honey, Milk, and Opportunities

The Book for Adult Education

From Scratch to Poor Section 8 to Ph.D.

By Elie B. Mbumina, Ph.D.

Empower Publishing
Winston-Salem

Empower

Publishing

Empower Publishing
302 Ricks Drive
Winston-Salem, NC 27103

First Empower Publishing Books edition published
November, 2025
Empower Publishing, Feather Pen, and all production designs are trademarks.

For Donations or Contributions, Readers may contact the author at PO Box 1235, Greensboro, NC 27402 or via mbuminae@aol.com, elie.contactchoir@gmail.com, or contact@evangelicalchoirandservices.com, or by calling (336) 988-0989 or (336) 202-6794

Cover design by Pan Morelli

Manufactured in the United States of America
ISBN 978-1-63066-623-1

Part 1

My Incredible Story of My Coming to America—A Land of Honey, Milk, and Opportunities

From Scratch to Poor Section 8 to Ph.D.

Introduction

Dear Readers, Friends and Countrymen!

I would like to express my gratitude to all of you for reading this book, for your interest in the subject matter, and your comments about what you have learned.

Indeed your contributions, donations or tokens will be dedicated to assisting the Christian Evangelical Churches founded since 1881. Also, a portion of these funds will be used for planting church buildings to be used for worship, Sunday School classes, Bible studies, and for assisting children with special needs, and helping the indigent.

I extend an invitation to any to any American and Canadian financial advisers to join me in coordinating these operations, regarding the budget, for this is important work. It is my hope that a percentage of the monetary contributions from this project will be used for the upbuilding of Evangelical Christian operations. All financial assistance will be greatly appreciated. May God bless you, bless all readers, bless Amazon and the owners, Madam Dr. Felecia Piggott-Anderson, my editor; Monsieur Baba Joseph Anderson, minister; and Mr. Jeff Bezos. God bless all the readers of this enriching story. God Bless America and the Democratic Republic of Congo (DRC)!

I would like to thank everyone who is willing to contribute by buying this book with the title *My Incredible Story of My Coming to America, A Land of Homey, Milk, and Opportunities.*

Elie B. Mbumina

Furthermore, I want to extend my thanks to those who are planning to support this project through monetary donations to cover the high cost of the publisher. I want to make sure that the sponsors' contributions will provide a fruitful and juicy result!

Surely, the book sales will reach many readers as possible, and they will learn a lot of valuable lessons from my travel and study-abroad experience. I hope that the next pages are going to bring you joy, laughter, entertainment, inspiration, and knowledge. It is my hope that actors and actresses in the United States will please support me and also make a movie with me about this incredible story!

Chapter 1
My Interesting Life in the Democratic Republic of Congo (DRC)

My name is Elie B. Mbumina, PhD, and this part of the story relates My Interesting Life in the Democratic Republic of Congo. The colonial powers changed the name of my country from Belgium Congo to Zaire and then back to Congo.

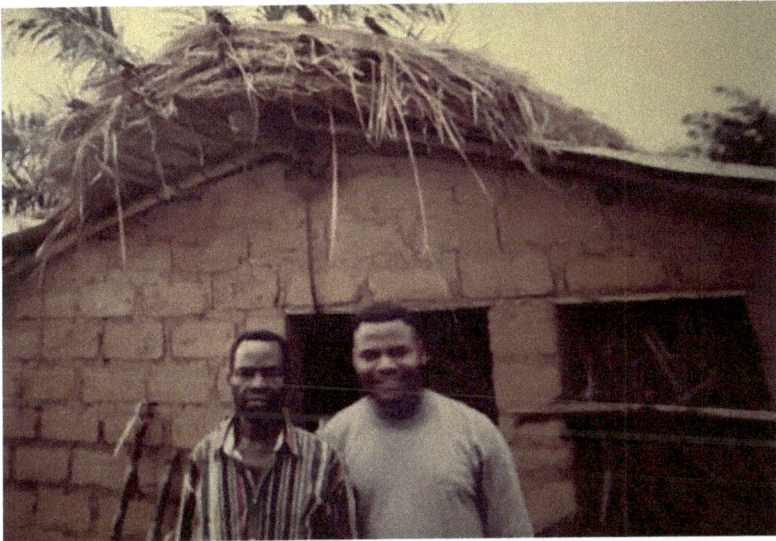

Elie with his father Elie standing before their home in the DRC, 1995.

I was born in the Democratic Republic of Congo, Africa and I spent my childhood with my parents, Mr. Elie Mbumina and Mrs. Helen Nzuzi. I have seven siblings—two brothers and five sisters—all born in the Democratic Republic of Congo (DRC), located in the center of Africa.

Elie B. Mbumina

What then made my family unique, special, popular, loved and attractive to virtually all? The answer is quite simple. First of all, both my parents, Papa Elie Mbumina and Mama Helene Nzuzi were born in the DRC in the 1930s. Unfortunately, during their early childhood, my Papa lost his mother and my Mama lost both of her parents.

Elie with his mother Helene.

Mama Helene Nzuzi is a twin, and her identical twin sister is named Albertine Nsimba. Please be informed that in my state of Bas-Congo in the Democratic Republic of Congo, twins carry very significant names. It doesn't matter whether the twins are boys or girls, the oldest is named Nzuzi, and the youngest is named Nsimba.

What caused the drama to both my beautiful, pretty, and smart twin mothers? And what has happened to my special Dad? Although both twins were indescribably geniuses, nobody could provide for their schooling. Therefore, the word about their lack of financial backing quickly spread all the way to the Swedish Missionary Schools in Sundi-Lutete. From there, the missionaries decided to adopt the oldest twin named Helene

4

Nzuzi, who is my mother. The youngest twin, Albertine Nsimba, could not be adopted because she was taking care of the youngest sibling Antoinette Nlandu.

In the 1950s, both my parents were grateful and lucky because they were educated at Swedish Evangelical Missionary School (EEMM-SMF) in Sundi-Lutete. In the entire school, my mother Helen Nzuri and Rebecca Mpola were the only two female students in the entire missionary school. The missionaries gave tremendously, financially, mentally, and materially to support the only two female students in the entire school. Also, my mother became a babysitter for Swedish missionaries and later for the other missionaries from Scandinavia, Belgium, England, Canada, the United States, and the American Peace Corps. Eventually the organization added more schools with different Christian church denominations, such as Baptist, Presbyterian, Lutheran, Pentecostal, and Methodist.

After graduation, my parents started their careers in education as instructors. Unfortunately, my father ascended to heaven about twelve years ago. However, my mother has been teaching more than seventy years. She cannot retire from her teaching job because Congolese government stole all the teachers' retirement funds. What a disgrace! Now my mother just continues to teach for her livelihood without the possibility of retirement.

It is so bad and sad to have a criminally corrupt, toxic political system in the Democratic Republic of Congolease! Please keep in mind that all teachers who worked so hard in the Congolese school system since the 1950s until the present, have never been paid even one dime for their retirement funds. The worst is that many of them died due to the stress, anxiety, high blood pressure, suicide attempts from working sixty to seventy years, but they get nothing at all for their retirements. What a horrible, terrible disgrace for them! They also suffer from malnutrition, exhaustion, and lack of clothing.

In the DRC, I spent over ninety percent of my entire life there in the Christian boarding schools. My mother taught me in first grade, and my father taught me in second grade on the elementary school level. Both of my parents were tough, severe and strict on disciplinary actions. They used the mix of corporal and vocal disciplinary methods for our education. I remember that my mother used to tell me, "Elie, never call me Mom in the classroom, but call me Madam Teacher Helene."

Their special teaching pedagogical methodology and psychology was very systematic, a combination of all educational methodologies which send clear messages and signals to all students by reminding all of us that the teachers are not only serious about us but they are focused on different future challenges for the learning process. They wanted to give us a solid foundation to make us the best that we could be. The strong motto was "Enter to learn and depart to serve." This same motto shines in front of Winston-Salem State University where I would later graduate in the United States. We know for sure that receiving knowledge, money, or service is good, but giving, sharing or providing a service to people is always better.

Chapter 2

At elementary school in Sundi Kimbonga, Democratic Republic of Congo, students had to study very hard to avoid repeating the school year. This school education system was set up early in the Nineteenth Century by the ex-colonial country Belgium and used before and after the independence on June 30, 1960.

From the third grade to the sixth grade, I moved to a different boarding school of Sundi-Mamba, Democratic Republic of the Congo. The only time I visited my family was on weekends, Saturday and Sunday. During that brief family visit, I helped my parents with household chores, agricultural projects, plantation work, and especially fishing work. At night, we would sit down around the storyteller to listen to those fabulous stories, proverbs, tales, and learn by drawing valuable lessons from them. Also, we used to hold hands together and sing different songs in a merry-go-round fashion. We had fun together during my home visits, but the disciplinary actions continued, and curfew was still enforced every night at 8:30 P.M. Everyone must be in bed by 9:00 P.M., without any exceptions. The corporal punishment was often reinforced as well. The moral and civic education level. started at a very early age. Learning how to do things correctly and appropriately was crucial. We students had to attend church services every week and we were required to pass the religion class in order to move to the next level.

After receiving my certification at the end of the sixth grade, I moved to a different school in Kinkenge, Democratic Republic of Congo, for my seventh and eighth grade called "Orientation Cycle" because the education system in DRC requires students to choose their future major related to their future job assignment before taking the state exam at the end of the eighth grade.

Elie B. Mbumina

I became heavily involved in choir, in soccer tournaments and in scout meetings and the dancing team. Even though I was having a lot of fun in this school, I had to make sure I was doing my schoolwork properly, efficiently and in a timely fashion because it seriously was no joke.

Due to the school load, materials, discipline, and the time constraints, I was going back at home only three times a year: Christmas, Easter, and at the end of the year in July. I remember watching my very first movie at the age of fifteen. It was a Swedish movie shown by the Swedish missionaries at school. The movie was called "Sweden in Winter." The film portrayed how the Swedish parents and their children loved the snow. During a heavy snowstorm, the children scooped up big bowls of snow under their snow tents. The children were playing in the snow, hitting one another with balls of ice and eating the snow like ice cream. The snow looked so cold, but oh so pretty! What an experience seeing a snow for the first time during my first movie!

Elie's parents before the Swedish Missionary School, 1960.

At the end of the eighth grade, after successfully passing my state exam, I was sent to Sona-Bata for my ninth through twelfth grade of High School called "Humanite-Secondaire." It was very interesting because we were taught by professors from different organizations and church denominations: American Peace Corps, Canadian missionaries; Dutch-Belgium missionaries; Egyptian professors; and Congolese professors.

In the DRC, there are about forty percent Catholic believers, fifty percent Protestant believers and ten percent of other religions. However, all denominations work together as a team. Student exchange is very common between catholic and Protestant schools. The liturgical exchange between pastors and choir members is tolerant between different church denominations.

The moral dimensions remain somewhat influenced or disconnected inside the school systems due to many factors, such as women's emancipation, equality between men and women, the conflict of interiority-complexity between genders, human rights, freedom of speech, equal opportunities, role of the activist, the role of the artist, and the like.

By comparing the current Congolese society with that of the 1960s, many rules have changed in schools, communities, and societies. For example, during the dating relationship, sex was avoided until the couple said their wedding vows. Sexual relations used to be a nice surprise by making love with different positions, for the first day or night after getting married.

The moral obligations once were requited to be stronger for many reasons: corporal punishment, obedience, drug restrictions, etc. . . . Waiting for marriage was a way to give respect to the women and mothers of the Congolese families. Despite these efforts in the past, the women in the Democratic Republic of Congo continue to become victims of many violent acts of discrimination, such as verbal abuse, domestic violence and date rape.

Chapter 3

My work experience in the Democratic Republic of Congo, which was Belgium Congo, then Zaire, and then back to Congo, was fulfilling.

After completing my high school education in Biology/Chemistry Concentration, I decided to move to Kinshasa, the DRC's capital, where I found my first teaching job. I completely understood and appreciated my school accomplishments after getting my first job and my first salary. I started to realize that educating children and families was very critical for the future of a community, society, and a country.

Citizens from Elie's village wade onto a boat to take them to Kinshasa, the capitol of the DRC, where they will purchase food and other necessities.

Overall, it became a moral obligation for me to be more appreciative to my parents, teachers, missionaries, church leaders, community leaders and society members for providing me the education, literacy training, spiritual life lessons I needed to equip me with the resources needed for my schooling. Most importantly, I do not take these opportunities for granted in the Congo or elsewhere. I stayed focused on my schoolwork, singing in the choir of the Congolese Evangelical Community, originally from Swedish Evangelical Missionary School (SMF) and extended to Congo since 1881, more than a century ago. I was also working on building construction on my vegetable gardens.

Preparing and Packing for my Long Adventure Trip to the Unknown Land – The United States of America Endeavor.

In 1980, I was thrilled to travel to the United States of America via Europe. My thoughts, conscience, and desire pushed me through to make a substantial move to the United States.

The close relationship that I had with the American Peace Professors and the Swedish and Belgium priests indeed heled me with a great deal to materialize my sweet dream.

I knew that I had to face many challenges ahead before and after leaving the DRC, but I was well-focused, mentally prepared with courage, hope, faith, prayer, commitment, dedication, determination, and perseverance.

I had so many questions about the unknown parts of the world, the United States, on one hand. On the other hand, I felt very proud and special about all my accomplishments as a young, dedicated, and committed person. Believing and trusting God and having confidence in myself led me to do extraordinary things. Becoming successful was the only choice.

In November 1980, I left Kinshasa, the Democratic Republic of Congo, previously called Zaire, on board of Air Zaire Boeing 747 to the United States of America via Brussels, Belgium. The first leg was an eight-hour flight. We left Kinshasa around 11:00 P.. After I ate dinner, my excitement mounted, but it quickly turned into a moment of anxiety and stress.

A woman sitting beside me on the airplane found out that I was having a difficult time. She struck up a conversation with me:

Q: Hey! What is your name? Are you O. K.?

11

Elie B. Mbumina

A: My name is Elie. Yes. I'm ok, BUT . . .

Q: But what? You are so young. Where are you going?

A: Well, I am going to the United States.

Q: Oh Yea! Is this your first time traveling to the U. S. A.?

A: Yes, indeed. But I have a week transit in Brussels before continuing to the U.S.A.

Q: OOOOH! Do you have friends or relatives in Brussels?

A: No. That's why I am a little bit scared.

Q: OOHHHH! My God! Are you a Christian?

A: Yes, I am. Also, my parents were raised and educated by the missionaries in the DRC.

Q: O.K. I see. Elie, listen. You are very nice, and if it is O.K. with you, I want you to stay with me and my other friends who are traveling with me in my family's house in Brussels. In addition, your food, lodging and transportation will be free of charge. Don't worry. We are going to take care of you, Babe, for the entire week. Also, I want you to know that I will take you to the Zaventem-Brussels Airport when you fly to the USA a week from now, O.K.?

A: Yes, Madame! Thank you very much! May God bless you and your family. What a huge relief for me! What a blessing! Frankly, that was a good indication and signal that my path and my trip were all set up by God. The highest God was in control, and I believed that God would never give me something that I could not handle.

During my stay in Brussels, I learned so much! I truly appreciated life, relationships, and humility. Humility made me such a good citizen of the world. I could not imagine the changes that were coming over me.

When I arrived in New York City in the United States, before landing at the John F. Kennedy Airport, I was so impressed with the skyscrapers, the highways, and the subways. Everything was so big in the United States compared to the environment in Europe and Africa. Since I was accustomed to speaking four different languages, including French, learning English as my fifth language was not quite as difficult as I thought.

12

My Incredible Story

At the J. F. Kennedy Airport, my interaction with the U.S. Immigration and Custom Officers was pleasant because I entered the USA with a solid English foundation, which I received from my American Peace Corps professors in the Democratic Republic of Congo (Zaire). My American professors included Professor Tina Thuermer, Professor Daniel Tamulonis, Professor Martha Brown, and Professor Amy Mellencamp. They are the greatest professors ever, of all time. The four language learning skills were taught so well: listening skills, reading skills, speaking skills, and writing skills. These four skills helped me to connect and reconnect with people during my flight to USA, during my conversations and interaction with people.

Again, upon my arrival to the United States of America, lively conversation and rich communication was made possible because I had excellent English professors in high school in Sona-Bata, Democratic Republic of Congo. They were the best in the world! One of them was Professor Daniel Fergus Tamulanis was his name, but we would call him by different names: "Mr. Dan" or "Professor Dan." He also taught us very good songs that we would sing during the holiday season.

Besides Professor Daniel F. Tamulanis, I had another excellent English professor named Professor Tina Thuermer. She was very young and beautiful. I remember the very first day, when she entered the classroom, almost everybody screamed out saying, "OOOOH! Oh la la!"

My math instructor, Professor Martha Brown, was outstanding and awesome!She was very patient to me and to all of us in general because math competencies do not come easily to everyone. Professor Jim Freeman was my other math teacher. Although we had a hard time understanding him at the beginning of the school semester, he made himself available to aa very engaging scholar and tutor.

My biology and chemistry instructor was Professor Rob Willis. He was excellent and very strict in the classroom. The very good news for him and for all other American Peace Corps instructors is that all students in the twelfth grade passed the state exam.

Elie B. Mbumina

These fantastic, terrific and wonderful American Peace Corps instructors, including Professor Amy Mellencamp, in Sundi-Lutute School and many more who worked in different departments, such as Mr. and Mrs. John Durgin, Mr. Tony Catino, Peace Corps Director, Mr. Jay Nash, Mr. Robert and Ms. Travis all had several characteristics in common—a good sense of hospitality, generosity, care, trustworthiness, and love.

During the holidays, the united States Ambassadors in the DRC, their staff, and the American Peace Corps used to celebrate together and some of my school colleagues and I were invited to those barbecue gatherings and parties. There was plenty of good food on the menu: fried chicken, hamburgers, cheeseburgers, baked ham, hot dogs, potato salad, macaroni and cheese, fried fish, green beans, baked beans, and drinks. We were treated so well! OH, Yes! What good times and unforgettable souvenirs!

Since the creation of the American Peace Corps in the 1960s by our famous U. S. President John F. Kennedy, the entire world became united around his brave ideas and thoughts to work hard and think well to accomplish something good. He said, "Every accomplishment starts with the decision to try."

Also, to express my gratitude to my Congolese and American teachers and professors, I keep following President J. F. Kennedy who said, "As we express our gratitude, we must never forget that the highest form of appreciation is not to utter words, but to live by them." What is more, Kennedy also said, " . . . Ask not what your country can do for you, ask what you can do for our country." These quotes will always fortify me by giving back as much as I can to the communities, societies and nations. Courage, hope, faith, motivation, and prayer continue to play an important role in my entire life. All days are not Sundays or gols because there are so many ups and downs to face, but one must keep going. For my dream of "My Coming to America" lifted me up and high.

After arriving in America and getting my United States Immigration and Customs straight, I caught my connecting flight

14

to Boston, Massachusetts, and I spent my very first night in America

There. At the Logan Airport, it already was dark outside. Two Americans—one male and the other female—saw me looking outside through the double doors. They came to me, greeted me, and asked me if I needed help. I told them, "Yes, indeed. I need help." With my best English, I explained my plight to them.

"I was supposed to visit some friends here in Boston, but I just discovered that my friends live too far from Logan Airport," I said. "Therefore, I need a place to sleep before continuing my route to Winston-Salem, North Carolina tomorrow. What am I going to do? I am so close, but too far away to meet them here tonight."

My two fellow Americans assured me that I should not worry because help is on the way.

"We have contacted one of the Logan Airport officers and explained your situation to him. They looked at your itinerary, and they have compromised to find you a hotel room, to arrange for your breakfast in the morning and for your transportation to the hotel and back to the airport tomorrow morning," said the American female.

With great joy, I said, "Thank you, my God! Thank you, Jesus! Thank all Americans for your generosity, hospitality and for your big hearts! Yes, America. How great you are!"

Before calling the shuttle to take me to the hotel, they placed a phone call to my relatives in Winston-Salem, North Carolina, to inform them about my arrival to the USA. Finally, I was looking forward to relaxing with the peace of mind that night at the hotel. Little did I know that after all of this back-and-forth confusion, I had one more rigmarole to go through that night.

I had a unique and humorous experience with the hotel shuttle that evening. On the way to the hotel, the shuttle driver also had to pick up a group of people from a wedding reception. One person in the wedding party was drunk, and he was releasing so many farts every five minutes in the van before our departure to the hotel! Nobody on the van could be comfortable with all of that human gas flying. After the first fart bombshell, the travelers and I kept all windows opened, but the bad smell was like pig and goat chitterlings mixed with chili beans or goat barbecue in peanut butter soup. One of the Americans riding with me suggested that the van driver take the farter and his relatives to the hotel first and them come back to take us to the hotel. But finally, it worked out well. We asked him to hold up his farts until we arrived at the hotel destination. The relatives compensated the driver with a good tip because of the faring man's troubles. He also apologized. The lesson I learned is that we are all human beings no matter where we go. We should have the courage to apologize for any of our bad actions, including filling the van with farts. Once we arrived at the hotel, I was able to check in, and I had a very peaceful night's sleep. God Bless. I was so grateful that God watched over all of the events of our day and brought us safely to our destination.

The next day, I flew from Boston, Massachusetts to Winston-Salem, North Carolina, via Charlotte, NC. Upon my arrival, my relatives, Dr. Victor Mayenge's family were ready at Smith Reynolds Airport in Winston-Salem, NC. What a warm welcome! I experienced troubles almost all night long, but today we are talking, laughing, earing and celebrating my arrival and most importantly "My Coming to America, the Land of Hope, Milk and Opportunity."

Chapter 4
My Tough Challenges, Determination and Perseverance in Completing My Education in the United States—Finding a Church, Friends, and My First Job

Completing my education in the United States of America was my main focus at all times. Coming with my broken English to the U.S.A., along with my courage, commitment, dedication, determination, focus, and perseverance, I studied English for only two months. Then I started taking my regular courses after successfully passing my English Placement Test at Winsalm Business College, which later became Rutledge College in Winston-Salem. In addition to that, my SAT Test was very difficult because I spent a very short time studying and preparing to take the test. Therefore, I barely passed it with a decent, acceptable score.

Adjusting and balancing my lifestyle in the United States was tough for the first few months because I had to pull myself together, keep up with good school grades, make new friends who were trustworthy, rely on bus transportation and other means, sign my lease and move into my own apartment, find the nearest grocery store, search for good hamburgers, barbecue, juicy steaks, pig feet, chicken livers, and chitterlings, and other dishes.

Fairchild Apartments was the very first apartment I moved into in 1981 in Winston-Salem, NC under Section 8. I felt so good about getting my own place, even though I could not afford a secondhand, dependable car. All I had in my apartment was my junk: a squeaky, noisy bed, one sofa that I picked up at a dumpster on the street. I had to clean it well to make sure that there were no dogs' fleas, lice, or crabs on the bed. Also, I had two cooking pans, a few groceries, serving spoons, a couple of clean sheets and bed spray. That is all I owned. I learned to drive.

17

Elie B. Mbumina

Moving to Winston-Salem, Elie became a student at
Winston-Salem State University in 1981.

I was working very hard to save money and buy a
secondhand, dependable car. After buying my little, old, red
Volkswagen, it was a big relief for me. Getting my driver's
license was an encouragement for me to buy a car and to drive
back and forth from my apartment to school, to the grocery store,
to church, and other places I needed to go. Sometimes, I did not
know how to handle some of my problems or troubles, because
I was lonely most of the time. Also, I was scared when I heard
from some people that I must find a girlfriend right away to live
with me. Finding a live-in girlfriend right away was not a part of
my plan.

I was among the few having more tough times in America
that many other ordinary immigrants because many of them
came to America just to work and make a living. However, I had
a goal of completing my college education and making a living
as well. You can imagine how challenging it can be when
somebody moves to a new country and a new continent. My
lifestyle completely changed in just a few days. I had to make a

quick adjustment, learning English as my fifth language, going to school and working two jobs, and adjusting from two seasons a year—rainy and dry—to four seasons a year.

Since I was coming from a Christian background, I was driving around to find a Christian church to worship in on Sundays. I did not care much about the denomination names because for me, members of Christian churches or Protestant churches, such as Baptist churches, Methodist Churches, Lutheran churches, Presbyterian churches, Pentecostal churches, or non-denominational churches are all Christians and children of God. I can worship and find fellowship with any of these believers.

At one point, I decided to find a make friends with people who I could sometimes spend good quality time with on the weekends. By doing that, I could meet a variety of people. One side, I could connect with a few church-going friends and family groups. On the other hand, I could also meet people who shared some of my social interests as well.

I previously met a young, beautiful girl named Juanita Price with her awesome, nice, and beautiful parents and friends. They included Mama Nancy, Papa Don, Mama Mary, and Papa Jim. They all helped me a lot for my living and studying in the United States. I appreciate and love them so much. She used to talk to me while washing my dishes at one local restaurant on Stratford Road in Winston-Salem called the Grinz Restaurant. I loved my first new job in America as a dishwasher. On Friday night, all cooks and staff, including me, were scrubbing the kitchen floor with hoses and water. We were doing this cleaning from 12:00 A.M. to 1:00 a.m. The owners of this restaurant, Mr. and Mrs. Smith, Mr. Lucky, and Mr. Mitch liked me so much because I was polite, and I was also doing a fantastic job, they said. I used to call them Mama and Papa Smith. The specialty of their restaurant was American-Mexican food. On Fridays and Saturdays, I was often dressed as a monkey puppet going to the bar and around the dining tables to dance.

African and American music styles! Wow! How the gyrations attracted the clients and customers! Also, Mr. Mark,

Elie B. Mbumina

one of the restaurant managers, taught me some profanity—words that I could use to talk with the clients at the bar and at peoples' tables English was still a new language for me. I thought that I was entertaining the people with Southern hospitality by using the following statements:

1. "Hey! Get the f—k off my way!"
2. "Hey, kiss my __ss!"
3. "Hey! (Sock) your tongue in there!"

My new friend Juanita was a regular customer at the restaurant, but she was shocked to see me running from table to table in a gorilla suit shouting such obscenities.

"Oh Elie, what the hell are you talking about? Please don't teach Elie to speak this way!" she said.

People were screaming, laughing and having a lot of fun when they heard me saying all of these phrases louder and louder with my foreign accent and my broken English. The restaurant was always full and packed on weekends to come to see me and hear my voice saying these humorous phrases. In fact, customers had to come early just to get a seat.

While working at Grinz restaurant during my first job in America, one day my car broke down and I needed a ride back home. One employee sent me to a waitress and told me to say to her, "My car f***** up, please take me home after work." Also he said to ask her if she needs a really good f*** and s***. The waitress screamed and came to the kitchen and she warned the employees in the kitchen to stop teaching me bad English words.

Frankly, I was not offended by anyone, and I did not know I was saying bad words or profane words to the many, many customers.

When I asked the clients what these words meant, they sent me back to Manager Mark to ask him. And when I asked him, he said, "They simply mean 'good stuff.' So Elie, keep it up! We really and truly love you! You are a very good man."

From the church side, my new friend Juanita who I met at Grinz Restaurant, invited me to go with her to church on the following Sunday. With happiness, I told her, "Yes, I would love to go to visit your church."

So after work at the Grinz Restaurant, she drove me back to my apartment that Saturday so she could find out where I was living. On Sunday morning, Juanita came to pick me up to go to church. When she arrived, she knocked at the door a couple of times because I had overslept due to the hard work, profanity speech and the dancing I was performing at Grinz Restaurant prior to that Sunday morning to attract clients, make them very happy, and boost profits as well. I let her in and she sat down and waited for me to take a quick shower and quickly got ready for church.

Testing the temperature of snow for the first time, Elie tries standing in it barefoot.

What a nice welcome surprise at church! Singing, praying, and listening to God's word was just awesome! Also, listening to the children's choir singing "Jesus Loves Me" was super! At the end of the church service, the pastor, the church members, and my lovely, sweet friend Juanita, all came over to meet me and shake my hand.

Juanita did a great job of introducing me to all the church members. She also asked me to go with her and her family have lunch at their house. The lunch was very delicious. We had soul food dishes, such as roast beef, fried chicken, potato salad, collard greens, macaroni, and cheese, corn bread, and red drink. I served myself twice since I was trying to recuperate from my night festivities. I surely regained some of my weight I lost

during my preoccupation with school and loneliness. I stayed at
their house that afternoon and took a good nap to get ready for
the evening church service. Then they took me back home. That
Sunday was a very special day for me. I felt good to become a
family member for my friend Juanita's family and the Church of
Christ.

*Winston-Salem, North Carolina, 1981: for the first time Elie
encounters snow.*

Mama Nancy and Papa Don are my friend Juanita's parents.
They adopted me in the USA as if I were their own child. They
helped me out when I enrolled at Winston-Salem State
University; they contributed to my tuition and fees, for my bills,
furniture and groceries. I spent a good quantity of time with them
on weekends and holidays. They always made sure that
everything was going well with me. They were truly my faithful
adoptive parents in the USA. They helped me out a lot
financially and spiritually with the Bible studies. They also were
my advisers who always made sure that I stayed out of trouble.

Overall, the entire Church of Christ was very supportive of
me with the Love of Jesus Christ that we all always shared. They
bought me clothes and shoes. I was invited several times to eat
breakfast, lunch or dinner with several church members. We

played volleyball sometimes after the church services and enjoyed pot luck for lunch. We also did some camping as well. I am so blessed, grateful, and humble to the entire Church of Christ membership. They were the first ones to welcome me to Winston-Salem, NC, USA. They fought so hard with the grace of God for me, my life, and for my education in the USA. It is a great honor for me to thank them. I greatly appreciate their generosity, support, and love.

I assisted and participated as an active member to another sister church called "Church of Christ." I was invited as a speaker to the Sunday School class to talk about the work the American, Canadian and Swedish missionaries did in the democratic Republic of Congo (ex-Zaire). Also, I was asked to talk about the lifestyle in Congo compared to the lifestyle in the Americas. It was very interesting for everyone. I compared four countries—the United States, Canada, Sweden and Congo—to provide more details as an insider and as an outsider. I also sang a solo in the choir for a long time there, and I was very grateful to be sponsored by Mama Petrou.

I met Mama Petrou, Mama Louise, Mr. Napleon, the custodian and floor manager, and Dr. Richards, a former professor at Wake Forest University in Winston-Salem, and Pastor Jerry. I honor them, especially Mama Petrou. Her son Mr. Omer, her daughter, Ms. Cathy, and hr granddaughter supported me so much at the university in the USA.

Dr. Handy, my dentist, and his wife invited me to attend Calvary Baptist Church in the 1990s. At that time, was also preparing to take my trip to the Congo to get married to my beautiful wife Faustina M. Mbumina. During those days, a group of missionaries from Calvary was preparing for a missionary trip to Africa. It was a perfect time for me to meet this team to share some of the ideas and details of the lifestyle in some African countries. Pastor Koch, Dr. Handy's family, and many Calvary Baptist Church members were very generous with a great sense of hospitality from the 1990s until now.

One of the best, perfect and lovely gifts I received from Dr. Handy's family was a brand new bed with a comfortable mattress just before my awesome wife Faustina arrived in the United States of America.

Just for your own information, the bed and mattress I received as a gift was so good and comfortable that I did not take a long time to impregnate my wife during our first play upon her arrival in the USA. What a good, long wedding night, especially keeping it up all night long!!

During his studies, Elie also got to spend time in Raleigh, the state Capitol of North Carolina.

Chapter 5
Balancing my Student Life, My Family, My Multiple Jobs and My Church Activities—"Enter to Learn. Depart to Serve."

When I was a single man in the 1980's and the 1990's, I was studying in Winston-Salem State University (WSSU), at North Carolina A & T State University (N.C. A & T), and at the University of North Carolina at Greensboro (UNC-G). I was studying for my Bachelor's degree in Business Administration and Economics at WSSU, for my Master's degree in Language Education at North Carolina A & T State, and then achieving my PhD in 2014 at Capella University and by consortium at UNCG, PhD in Professional Studies.

Between the 1980's—1990's, it was quite a turbulent moment for me in adjusting my life in the United States. I was living by myself under Section 8 policies at Fairchild Apartments in East Winston-Salem. This neighborhood was known as apartments for poor people or very low-income dwellers. We are all aware of the conditions under which many people live in the Hood: some of them are addicted to drug and alcohol problems.

The word spread quickly that there was a new guy in town who recently came from Africa who is now living at Fairchild Apartments. This fresh news brought a curiosity to almost all ages – young African American girls, boys, and young adults as well. I became so popular! I was a source of attraction, a source of interest and curiosity.

People around me revealed a mix of feelings. They started to follow my steps and ask me surprising, incredible questions. The conversation below sheds light on their comments and reactions. Black males in the community asked most of these questions, and some of them are very ridiculous!

Elie B. Mbumina

1. Q. Hello . . . Hey . . . Hi . . .
   A. Hello Madam . . .Mademoiselle . . . Sir . . .
2. Q. What is your name?
   A. My name is Elie.
3. Where are you from?
   A. I am from the Democratic Republic of Zaire (Congo).
4. Q. Oh, by the way, where is Zaire located? It must be in the Bahamas or somewhere, right?
   A. Of course not.
5. Q. How did you come to America? By car or by train?
   A.Oh yes! I came to America from Congo by airplane. You can't get there by car or train.
6. Q. Oh yeah! How long did it take you to drive or go by train from Congo or somewhere like that . . . to the United States?
   A. Ohooooo, no! You cannot drive from Congo, Africa to the USA.
7. Q. Shit! Why is it not possible to drive from Africa to America, Man?
   A. You can't because of the sea or the ocean. You cannot drive across these large bodies of water. You will have to travel by airplane.
8. Q. How long did you fly from your country Africa to USA?
   A. Africa is not a country, but it is a big continent. Europe is a continent! Asia is a continent! North America is a continent. Oceania is a continent. Therefore, the Democratic Republic of Zaire (Congo) is located inside and in the center of Africa. It takes eight hours to fly from Congo to Brussels, Belgium, Europe, or to Paris, France. Then it requires possibly eight to ten more hours including your flight connections to your final destination. Therefore, in total, it may take sixteen hours to eighteen hours of travel.
9. Q. In Africa, do you wear clothes or leaves?
   A.What question is this? Please watch the news or travel to Africa.
10. Q. In Africa, do you have houses of just jungle forests?

A. Please visit or revisit the fight of Muhammad Ali and George Foreman. Sir or Madam, did you learn geography at school?

11. Q. Damn! So did you come with your girlfriend or your wife?

A. No. I came to America by myself.

12. Q. Oh. Nah! Why didn't you bring your girlfriend or somebody with you to America, man?

A. Because this is an incredible adventure in the first place. Then I set up my priority goal which is completing my education in America first before getting involved in a serious relationship with a woman.

13. Q. Yes, but you seem to be a Black Man in good shape. man, you may need to do some things with a woman. So you haven't found the one for you yet? She or her mom will cook for you, right?

A. No. not yet Sir/Madam. Also, I have to cook myself instead of depending on somebody. I have to take responsibilities.

14. Q. Elie! You see that there are so many women over here in America! Which lady do you want to get with?

A. I don't understand your question Sir/Madam!

15. Q. I mean do you like a woman with a big butt or medium or small size or extra large size?

A. Oh please! I don't know yet. I am shy!

16. Q. Elie! Don't become shy! That is not like men! So what about breasts? To keep you warm, what is your preference? Big size, medium size, small size, or extra large ones?

A. Please, I just got here in my incredible coming to America. I am trying very hard to avoid being confused about these distractions and entertainments, at least for now. You see, I am afraid these may derail my main goals and objectives!

17. Q. Hey Elie, do you like a tall, a medium, or a short height woman?

A. I think height does not really matter. But it is the conduct that counts, her behavior, her religious faith, and love.

Elie B. Mbumina

18. Q. You know, this is America. It is not Africa. Therefore, you need to find a girlfriend as soon as possible. Do you understand?

A. Yes. I understand. But I need more time to get settled here first.

19. Q. O.K. Quick question. In Africa, do you eat special kinds of food? If yes, how? Here we have many crocs (crocodiles) who eat people by using a tongue in there!

A. Yes. In Africa and in Congo, we eat many different kinds of food.

20. Q In Africa, do you eat monkeys, snakes and escargot?

A. Personally, I don't eat those dishes, but some people in Africa do.

21. Q. In Africa, do you smoke reefer, marijuana, or pot?

A. Yes, some people do, but not me. It grows naturally very strong.

22. Q. In Africa, do they cut women's clitorises off to circumcise them?

A. No. Not in my country, Congo.

23. Q. Hey. Listen. In Congo and Africa, do you eat pussy? If yes, how do you eat it? And how does it taste? Does it taste like salt or candy or butter, or something else?

A. Oh, come on! Why do you ask these stupid, embarrassing and personal questions? No and no answer because I don't know.

24. Q. Hey! What about penis enhancement using a hot towel, soap and water to wrap your penis and let the milk seep out? This technique will improve your penis size, and it is a great warm-up exercise.

A. No please stop! Leave me alone!

25. Q. In Africa, when making love, do you use horse or dog or chicken or women on top or the missionary position? Which position do you like the most?

A. Madam/Sir, I came to America as a virgin. So I don't know.

28

Chapter 6

My first awesome discovery during my orientation night for training and graduation was related to my sexual activities, since I was a virgin at this time.

During my incredible coming to America, the impact was immeasurable. I went through a great deal of anxiety and hard times:

1. I experienced a great deal of pressure attempting to complete my college education, which was my primary goal.

2. I had to search and find a suitable, permanent job to be able to pay for my tuition and fees for my scholarly pursuits and to pay for my living expenses in America.

3. In order to find a job and secure my driver's license, I had to master the English language. I also needed this knowledge to buy a car, to drive back and forth to campus, to drive home and to drive to work.

4. In order for me to survive difficult times, I had to acquire a few good friends to talk to during my leisure time and during times of hardship.

5. Dealing with my social life, I often explained my sexuality or my virginity to various people I met.

One night, my beautiful girlfriend came into my apartment to study for her exams. She brought some snacks, soda, and beers, such as Bull and Old English. She said: "Elie, I don't know which drink you like better, but you can try both of them."

I said to her: "Thank you Madam and let me try all of them. As you know, alcohol goes very well with snacks."

I started drinking without realizing that Bull and Old English beers are very tough, very and they contain a very high percentage of alcohol. I knew myself that I was not an alcohol consumer nor a hard drinker.

Elie B. Mbumina

About thirty minutes later, my head started to stir. I became impacted by the beverage with extraordinary courage. Because of the extraordinary courage, my shyness went away. I started to sing in French to my girlfriend, sharing some love songs and soul songs. I stood up and started to dance. Then I started to touch her, to turn her on too! When the entertainment started to heat up, she called my name and asked me if I were okay. I replied by saying: "Yes, Madam! I am okay, but I feel like I need something."

Follow this summary:

Girlfriend: "Elie, are you okay?"

Me: "Yes Madam. I like you and love you! You are Ooooh lalalalalalaaaaaaa!

Girlfriend: "Thank you. I love you too, Elie!"

Me: "Please, may I ask your permission?"

Girlfriend: "A permission? Go ahead."

Me: "May I touch you please?"

Girlfriend: Elie, you are so polite by asking me a permission! Yes, go ahead."

Me: "Thank you, Madam. I love it!"

Girlfriend: "Well, I see you need something special from me. Right?"

Me: Yes, but still am shy because this is my first time in life to do it."

Girlfriend: What!? What do you mean the first time? You never tried a girl?

Me: "No. I am a virgin."

Girlfriend: "What! Are you serious? You are 25 years old! But your pants are showing that you are ready!"

Me: "Yes indeed, but I don't know how to start because I want to heat this up right now. Oh yes, Madam!"

Girlfriend: "Okay, Baby. I love you so much because you are attractive, nice, polite, and very honest with me. Don't worry. I will teach you, okay?"

Me: "Yes! Thank you, Madam. Let's go!"

My Incredible Story

Girlfriend: "Are you ready to throw down? Go ahead with a gentle touch and eat like a hungry man. Yes, keep it up until you finish it up! Don't stop Baby! How do you feel?"

Me: "OOOh LAlala! Madam! I feel sooooo goooooooood! You make me scream of joy, pleasures, and love! Oh, you speak the unknown tongue!"

Girlfriend: "Yes, Honey. You really did an excellent job. You make me speak the unknown tongue because you make me happy. You now graduate, my love. Keep up the good job."

Overall, my college experience in the United States was not only interesting but a good one as well. It was up and down. Sometimes I felt like being in the middle of nothing and nowhere with loneliness. But most of the time, I was I the middle of good people. I was very well coached, advised, and taken care of my many good and outstanding professors faculty members, parents, ordinary people, and staff members.

During the years 1983 until 1987, Winston-Salem State University (WSSU) became my home institution. After coming from the Democratic Republic of Congo (DRC) with my English language style limitations I thought that the ASAT was the only qualified determinant to enter WSSU. But I was supposed to go through the placement tests and many more challenges. Thank God that I overcame these even when being exempted from a couple of courses. My freshman year at WSSU was more difficult because I had to make many adjustments to my class, living space, work schedule, and social life.

Even though my English proficiency was not high, I was taking a full load—fifteen to eighteen hours of credits per semester. It really was very hard to balance all that and take care of my job, bills, school, library assignments, and myself. I had to double, triple and quadruple my efforts because I wanted to finish my four-year college experience on time—from 1983-1987. So I did.

My sophomore and junior years were all much better than expected. Besides the school's rigorous curriculum, I was having a good time partying in the student union and in the gym on

31

Friday and Saturday nights. I felt that I was also able to test and enjoy campus life with my colleagues on weekends. I learned to dance American music mush such as Soul, slow music, Rock and Roll and Disco. Every year during my college time, I was invited by American families to celebrate with them for New Year's, Easter, Fourth of July, Thanksgiving, and Christmas. They were so nice with their hospitality.

My senior year at WSSU was somewhat easier, but I had to do a lot of research papers, presentations, group studies, tests, and several final exams before graduation. I had no time to waste. Since it was my last year before earning my Bachelor's degree. I decided to go on school excursions and camping trips with my classmates to Ridgecrest Mountains, Mount Airy in Pilot Mountain to the games and to the beaches. During these trips, we used to make many stops on the road to buy homemade ice cream, fresh, green peanuts, vegetables and fruits. What a great feeling being among my fellow Americans! My spirit was truly boosted up in the American communities and society. Just keep in mind for twelve consecutive years, I was the only Congolese studying at Winston-Salem State University. Also, I was the only one in the entire city. I was making sure that I had an adequate, dependable transportation source because living by myself, working a full-time and a part-time job, and then being a full-time student with fifteen to eighteen credit hours was really getting on my nerves. But I was getting a lot of encouragement from the people who told me to hand in there.

My first graduation after four years matriculating for my Bachelor's degree took place in May of 1987 at Winston-Salem State University. It was awesome! I was marching with my professors, staff members, relatives, and fellow students, and we were all engulfed by joy and happiness! What a special moment in time. Relatives and friends made me feel so good! I received gifts of encouragement that included monetary blessings. What pride! What joy!

In 1987, Elie Mbumina graduated from WSSU.

I cried with emotions when the graduation song played. It was a sunny day with clear skies. Friends and relatives showed up at the Winston-Salem Coliseum. They screamed, sang, shouted, and applauded with all happiness. They congratulated me. I really and truly felt so good after completing this endeavor. My work, commitment, dedication, determination, and perseverance paid off! Thank you, God!

We took lots of pictures for my graduation. We celebrated this auspicious occasion with an awesome party. I called back home in the DRC and chatted with my parents and extended family members. They welcomed this wonderful news! They celebrated with a distinctive joy, and they gave thanksgiving to God. Thank you, Jesus!

Elie B. Mbumina

Elie, the scholar, matriculated first at Winston-Salem State University.

Chapter 7
A Poem and a Love Song for Winston-Salem State University

After my graduation at Winston-Salem State University, I started to feel nostalgic for saying, "Goodbye WSSU." I composed a poem or song that I dedicated.

"Winston-Salem State University, My Belle, My Mission and My Love I send this poem with my kindest, best and warmest regards:

Thank you, thank you, thank you WSSU!

What a beautiful journey and endeavor at WSSU.

You accepted me, welcomed me, and educated me.

OOOOOHHHHHHHHHH WSSU, how excellent and kind you In 2010, I became heavily involved in working on my PhD

35

Elie B. Mbumina

in Professional Studies (Education). The combination of my credentials, classes and teaching and working experiences led me to the highest achievement, PhD with grades coming from all of the many universities I attended: Winston-Salem State University, North Carolina Agricultural and Technical State University, the University of North Carolina at Greensboro, and Capella University.

are.

WSSU, my BELLE, my MISSION and my LOVE,
How wonderful and magnificent you are.
Yes, I will remember the hard work and parties.
WSSU my SWEETHEART and awesome INSTITUTION.
You milked me, you honeyed me beautifully.
Oh yes, you will always stay in my humble heart.
Yes, it is just a goodbye, not a farewell. I love you.

While studying and working on my Bachelor's of Science degree at Winston-Salem State University (WSSU), I accepted a job offer from Sara-Lee Hanes Company. We were making men's and women's products, such as t-shirts, stockings, panties, and hats, etc. I selected third shift to give myself enough time for my studies at WSSU. However, the most common problem for the third shift position was my getting too tired and sleepy in my classes.

For example, one day I was very sleepy in my classroom, and I was still sleeping on my chair until my professor came and awakened me. My professor was very disappointed that I was asleep during his lecture. I apologized immediately.

At the Sara-Lee Company, I met so many women who would talk to me and socialize with me on the job and after hours. I also met good male friends, but the problem with them was that they were teaching me how to use profanity in the English language so that they could laugh about the sound of it.

For example, one of the favorite songs that one of my male friends taught me to sing to women was, "Do it! Do it! I wanna do it to youuuuuuuu!"

Ohhh! Men!! Women became very upset with him by telling him, "Please, Elie is a cool young man. Don't you teach him bad

36

language. Please, Elie, ignore him and forget what he is teaching you, they said.

After getting my Bachelor's degree at Winston-Salem State University, I headed up for my Master's degree in foreign languages at North Carolina Agricultural and Technical State University and at the University of North Carolina at Greensboro, where I was taking classes in Higher Education. We had few professors from the University of North Carolina at Chapel Hill commuting back and forth from Chapel Hill, NC to Greensboro, NC. What a full load of the classwork for me!

Elie received his Master's Degree from North Carolina A&T University in Greeensboro.

Elie B. Mbumina

Also, I was working three jobs: one full-time job teaching French and working in the Foreign Languages Laboratory at North Carolina A & T State University; one part-time job as American Express NROC Greensboro, NC; and at AMEX, I was handling a very high calls volume for French-Canadian in the province (state) of Quebec, Canada. Also, I was making welcome phone calls for the customers for English speakers in Canada, especially in the provinces (states) of Ontario, British Columbia, Alberta, Manitoba, new Brindswick, etc. . . and calling USA-Canada. USA-Canada American Express customers for Anti-Attrition program, to educate and encourage people on how to use their AMEX card and get the most of it.

When my manager and supervisors at American Express found out that I was getting too many complimentary phone calls from clients who were saying that I was doing such a fantastic, awesome job, they both came to me and talked to me about it. They congratulated me and told me that my hard work makes American Express very proud because my customer service attracts to many customers to apply for the American Express green, gold, Optima, Delta Sky miles and company (corporation) cards.

Therefore, American Express asked me to get another training for setting up pin numbers electronically—online for people traveling locally, nationally, or internationally in all five world continents: North America, South America, Africa, Asia, Europe, and Oceania. I did all of these with joy, courage, and humility.

By seeing me perform all these many jobs during the three-day shifts, many people became amazed, anxious and astonished because they worried so much about me because I was not sleeping at all during some days. They were asking most of these questions:

1. Q. "Elie, do you ever sleep or go to bed?"
   A "Yes, but I do not get enough sleep."
2. Q. "Why do you not sleep enough?"
   A. "Because I am working three jobs."
3. Q. "Why do you work so many jobs?"

38

A. "Because I love to take care of my family and school."

4. Q. "Do you ever get tired, or disoriented because of too many jobs?"

A. "No, but I feel exhausted sometimes."

5. Q. "Elie, do you have an African Lion energy?"

A. "No. I have courage, commitment, perseverance, hope, faith, and prayers that motivate me the most to accomplish what I need to do."

After my wedding, I had three children, including a set of twins—Karen, and Kevin, Howard, and a wife. I was working three jobs and going to school full-time. This schedule was very tough, but thank God that I was able to manage it all.

In 2005, Elie traveled to Atlanta, Georgia, where he visited the Martin Luther King, Jr., Memorial (above) and had the pleasure of sitting on the front step of Dr. King's home (below).

Elie B. Mbumina

I also attended many workshops and three university colloquiums in Anaheim, Orange County, California, Dallas Texas, and Atlanta, Georgia. Working on my comprehensive exams and my dissertation were huge challenges. These tasks were like headaches and seemed like my own my personal hell. But I had excellent American professors, advisers, counselors, and mentors that I will never forget during my whole life. With victory in Jesus, I earned my PhD in May of 2014.

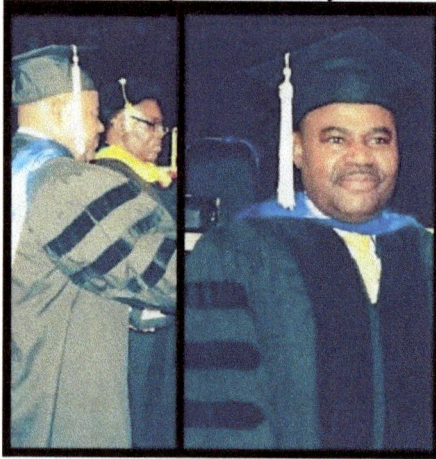

Elie receives his PhD from Capella University, 2014 As part of his PhD process, Elie made a graduation speech in May, 2014..

Conclusion:
**My Incredible Coming to America with My Motto.
"Enter to Learn; Depart to Serve.
And the Legacy Continues" with Hope, Faith,
Love, Commitment, and Perseverance.**

My voyage, adventure and journey to the United States of America is a fruitful, novel and very successful experience by the grace of God, the assistance of my professors, my family members, and my fellow Americans. My MISSION, my VISION and my DREAM were very well accomplished.

My mission of coming to America is gorgeously compared to the astronauts flying in space with the Shuttle to discover with conscientious effort the moon and the other stars.

My vision of coming to America is distinctively compared to a golden eagle flying in horizons to see very far away the world in which all human beings, including all creatures, live. What an amazing grace in the world!

My hope, faith and prayer lead me to a comparison of "Victory in Jesus," the Son of God. The Holy Spirit accompanied me from the Democratic Republic of Congo (Zaire) via Europe to the United States of America to acquire, complete and practice my full intellectual potential. From Scratch to Section 8 to Ph.D., to professor, to interpreter, to translator, to missionary, to world traveler, to a writer to professional communities and societies, to a national and international server and to a world traveler to five continents: North America, South America, Africa, Asia, Europe and Oceania. Oh America! How Great You Are! God Bless!

Over the years, Elie has visited Washington D.C. on multiple occasions, first in 1989. He has met a number of noteworthy leaders, including Presidents George H.W. Bush and Ronald Reagan.

Part 2

MY FIRST SIN DURING A DATE WITH A WOMAN WHEN I STILL WAS A VIRGIN AT THIRTY. WHAT WENT WRONG? WHAT HAPPENED? AND WHY SO CRAZY?

"BEING SWEPT OFF MY FEET—FROM TOE TO HAIR!" EDITORIAL

Dear Awesome Readers,

Before I capture your close attention to this honest but incredible story, I would like to thank each of you for your genuine support in buying this exceptional and interesting book. Also, those who are planning to support through monetary donations to cover the high costs of the publisher, I truly and sincerely greatly appreciated your support.

As you know, in order to educate the next generations, we need to emphasize details of an autobiography with honesty, sincerity and courage as we express what we go though in our lives. I was once a very shy person until I emigrated to the United States of America. However, I found out during my travel, study and socio-living personal experiences that these details may become excellent tools to teach others about the realities of life that I face every single day. Education must prevail because it is the key. Education allows all of us to move forward.

Stories and history may be good to tell, but they remain the way they are, and we realistically prefer not to change the truth. These types of stories frankly often contain painful events;

therefore, readers have to maintain patience, perseverance and courage in order to deal with these facts objectively.

Furthermore, I am quite sure that readers, wherever they are, will learn from my previous life experiences. Those who read this text in the future will also glean didactic lessons from this autobiography. It is my hope that as you read the next pages, they will intensify your joy, supply you with entertainment, and endow you with new ideas, knowledge and positive thoughts as well as fresh learning experience that we all need. Certainly, I cannot forget to thank AMAZON and the owners of AMAZON, Mr. JEFF BEZOS, and MADAME DR. FELECIA PIGGOTT-LONG and BABA JOSEPH ANDERSON.

Dear MOVIE STARS and ACTORS in the United

Would you please support me and make a movie with me about this incredible story? Your participation will be greatly appreciated.

CHAPTER 1
INTRODUCTION

I came from the Democratic Republic of Congo (DRC) with a background as a church missionary. I grew up in a large family. My parents raised not only us (their own children) but they also raised their nieces, nephews, and other close relatives in the same house. Since my parents had a good sense of hospitality, generosity, and love for others, they worked very hard as teachers and farmers. They taught in the mornings and early afternoons. During the evening hours, my parents had to run to the farms, to tend cattle, chicken and fish tanks as parts of our family businesses.

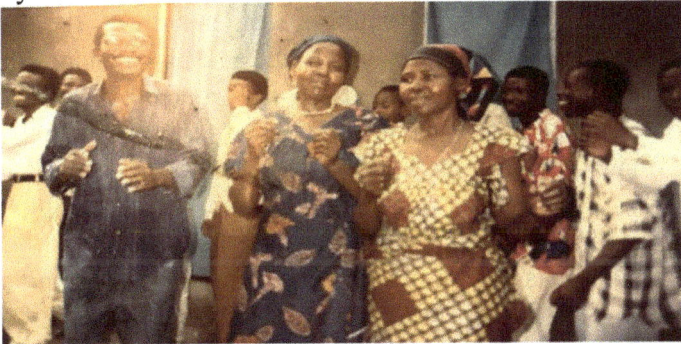

Elie's family and church members sing to celebrate his return to the DRC at Christmas, 1995.

My parents implied the expression of "teaching people how to fish instead of providing fish for them all the time." They taught us how to fish, to work on farms, to raise chickens, pigeons, ducks, goats, ships, pigs and cows. We never ran out of food or experienced starvation at home. My Papa and Mama, who we call Dad and Mama, who we call Mom, always made sure that we had enough food in our home. Therefore, the role of the family is very critical in the Congolese Society. The moral choices, civic behavior, family responsibility, and education are

Elie B. Mbumina

very important. Our parents taught us to respect ourselves and others to show ourselves friendly to people we meet.

Overview of My Origin Country
The Democratic Republic of Congo

The Democratic Republic of Congo, formerly known as Zaire, is located in the heart, or center of Africa. The equator line crosses the country and splits it into two parts. The large forest, which some call "jungo" is found across the equator line. The Democratic Republic of Congo (DRC) is a big, immense, rich country with 2,345,000 square kilometers of land. The population is about 100 million. The density is about fifty inhabitants per square kilometer. Most people are in the rural exodus from the small villages and centers to the large cities.

The Democratic Republic of Congo is bordered on the northwest by the Congo Republic; to the north by the Center African Republic and Sudan; and to the east by Uganda, Ruanda and Burundi. To the south, the DRC is bordered by Zambia and Angola. Kinshasa is the capital and the largest city. Even though the official language is French, there are also four national languages spoken in the DRC. They are Lingala, Kikongo, Swahili and Tshiluba.

The DRC has hot, humid, and cool weather. The temperature varies between 24 and 30 degrees centigrade (60 degrees – 85 degrees Fahrenheit). It is very humid during the days and nights. Most of the parts of the DRC have two seasons a year. The rainy season—from October 15 to May 15—and the dry season—from May 15 to October 15—marks the seasonal variation.

The Democratic Republic of Congo has some of the richest soil in the world. The DRC has a limitless water supply flowing from the world's second largest river, the Congo. The most important minerals are coltan for the fabrication of the electronic devices such as telephones, computers, and the software market. Other very important mineral resources are uranium, cobalt, copper, diamonds, gold, oil, wood and coffee. Because the DRC is classified as the richest country in the world when it comes to mineral resources, and peace, security and stability are very difficult to achieve there. Almost all countries in the world want to settle down in the DRC to establish cooperations and businesses.

The DRC was an ex-Belgian colony before its independence in June 30, 1960. President Joseph Kasa-Vubu was the first president of the Democratic Republic of Congo, followed by President Joseph Desire' Mobutu in 1965, then President Laurent Desire/ Kabila in 1997. In 2001, came President Joseph Kabila and President Antoine Tshisekedi in 2018.

The very sad, horrible and terrible problems for the Democratic Republic of Congo are rapes, massacres, crimes, balkanization, occupation and incontrollable corruption, malnutrition, starvation, illiteracy due to the corrupted system and non-government adequate governing structures, inflation, currency devaluation and eroded transportation means and system.

It was a blessed occasion when Elie's mother Helene visited the U.S. and met with church members.

CHAPTER 2
LIFESTYLES IN THE
DEMOCRATIC REPUBLC OF
CONGO

Teenagers and Dating Customs

In the 1950's and the 1960's, the teenagers and the dating customs were very different from today. Many changes have occurred in the communities and societies due to women's emancipation, women's rights, "no woman left behind," regarding women's and men's equality and education.

Sexual intimacy was considered as a welcome surprise between a man and a women during their wedding night. In the Democratic Republic of Congo (DRC) in particular, and in many African countries before the 1960's, it has been common that most men and women had remained virgins up to the evening of their honeymoons.

Sexual intimacy was considered as a welcome surprise between a man and a woman during their wedding night. In the Democratic Republic of Congo (DRC) in particular, and in many African countries before the 1060;s, it has been common that most men and woman had remained virgins up to the evening of their honeymoons.

However, two challenging questions remained. How does the groom find out the virginity of the woman during the wedding night? Also, what happens if the women is not found to be a virgin during the first night of making love with her brand-new husband?

These two questions can be very disturbing ones because it was very difficult to talk about sexual activities between young people. Seeing this as a taboo subject, parents, extended family members, and other ordinary people have made many mistakes

48

by offending the brides and grooms because of this sensitive issue. On the one hand, some spouses wanted to talk about sex, but on the other hand, others tried very hard to suppress the conversation, to avoid talking about it.

In fact, finding the answer to the first question, or determining the virginal status of the brand-new wife is during the very first day or night of the intensive and heavily sexual activities was quite simple. This is how it worked and how it was done:

The aunt on the paternal (father) side was cleverly playing double roles for the newly- married couple on the wedding night. The first role was to teach the unexperienced couple how to have sex or how to make love by using as many different positions as they can. The second role of the paternal aunt was to check and verify if there were blood in the private part of the new wife after the sexual performance.

Finding blood into the private part of the new wife was a good signal testifying that she indeed married as a virgin. Then it was an honor and a celebration for the small and extended family. This form of investigation harks back to the Old Testament practice that takes place in Deuteronomy 22:13-21.

The answer to the second question is also connected to this scriptural reference. If the new wife was not found showing evidence of being a virgin—meaning if there was not blood in her private body part, the aunt will run outside the house to inform people that this new wife was already deflowered by another man or by her husband before traditionally getting married. What a shame for her, for her small and extended family, and for other associated people or for her friends!

But one thing is certain! All these rituals were not always telling the correct results because the woman's body can go through many biological changes during her adolescence or puberty. Who knows? Guilty or not guilty, there was no medical or scientific proof of her virginity. In some cases, it was a horrific, disgraceful and disgrace procedure many women endured. If the family were to follow the biblical law to the letter, the woman would be stoned to death because she has tempted to "play the whore in her father's house." However, because of the grace of God, and the gift of forgiveness God granted through His Covenant, "If the Son therefore shall make you free, you shall be free indeed" (John 8:36).

As I mentioned before, the expert aunt was also playing an important role of teaching the new couple how to make love using different positions. Included among these positions are the missionary position (ordinary position), chicken, dog or horse position, sitting- down position, standing-up position, banding position, and the sleeping-on-side position.

However, the new couple needs to go though this sexual training process and test until the aunt graduates and congratulates them by telling them and by confirming the family members that they are now ready to go on their own. This successful sexual ceremony is literally followed by a big celebration with delicious fellowship meals. For example, they may be served barbecue goat, goat burgers, goat steak, lamb barbecue and sauce, chicken, fish, vegetables, fufu and plantain.

The follow-up for this sexual training and graduation may take place for several days just to ensure that everything is acceptable with the young married couple. What a positive impact this sexual training session played in the future life of the new couple!

This sexual training session, testing and followed by the graduation ceremony will help the newly-married couple to mutually enjoy themselves. This process also comforts, encourages and prepares them to cleave to one another all of their life and helps them to avoid or prevent cheating outside their marriage. If the new couple is well trained, it will literally be very difficult to talk about the lack of sexual satisfaction or divorce. Of course, each day is not Sunday, nor is everything always roses for the couple. They must face the vicissitudes of life, or the ups and downs with sexual temptation, but the chances of staying together their entire life will be greater than the desire to part ways..

Also, just keep in mind that in case of conflicts between the new couple, the small family and the extended family will step in to assist them. In some instances, their close friends or church members may also intervene. But prayerfully, the small conflicts will not escalate into extreme dramas.

There are also negative reactions and impacts of the sexual training session, testing and sexual graduation ceremony. By comparing and contrasting the past and the present generations, today this new millennial generation in the Democratic Republic of Congo in particular and in Africa generally, I have discovered that the majority of young teens, adults and elders to not like nor appreciate these sexual ritual ceremonies. According to their reflections, these traditional rituals bring so many negative effects not only on an individual's mind but also in the entire community, society and whole country.

Polygamy and Polyandria for Example:

The young man or the young woman may become shy, shame or traumatized during the rest of his or her life. The supervision of the sexual activities by the aunt during the first day or night of marriage may also affect the sexual performance of one or the two married individuals morally, physically, or spiritually.

Therefore, these strange sexual ritual ceremonies are dramatically disparaging in the communities, societies and countries.

Of course, nobody wants to be investigated or supervised during their moments of intimacy, while having sex with their new spouse. No one appreciates seeing his or her aunt screaming beside the bed by calling his or her name while telling the person what to do.

For example, some aunts have yelled out the following directives: "Put your wife on top!" "Put your wife on the bottom!" Make slower movements by dancing and singing!" "To the left!" "To the right! To the right!" "Push up! "Push Up! "Push up!" "Get down!" "Get down!" "Go deeper!" "Now dance really good!" "Push hard like a man!" "Let's go and dance: North—South—East—West—North—South—East—West,

51

Hit—Hit—Hit—and Hit hard! Oh yes—Oh yes—Oh lala!——
—Oh yes—-Oooh lala!"

In today's modern societies, sex therapy is administrated by education, reading, counseling, moral and civic education, media, Christian education and seminars.

Separation, Divorce and Reconciliation

Separation in the 19th century was less frequent between the couples than it is in the 20th century. Arguments, disputes and quarrels or escalations were more controllable by the couples due to the family ties, better moral and civic education provided by the preceding generations as well as the religion influences in the communities, societies, and the nation.

The divorce rate also was very low in the 19th century because of the good education given by parents who were in most cases the role models. It was always easier to settle the conflicts between the couples even for those who were victims of arranged marriages. If the difficulties persist inside the marriage, the minister and the missionary counseled the couple by coaching the couple. This was very similar case to my personal experience since I (Elie) am one of those who was involved in an arranged marriage in the Congo.

Reconciliation has always been a crucial step for couples who experience brokenness during their marriage. The goal is to assist them so they can progress with their normal marital life. However, the most difficult challenge for the reconciliation in many marriages in the Congo is that sometime the couples may run into a situation where too many people, friends, or relatives interfere in their marriage. In this case, too many counselors can confuse the couple.

For example, since too many people cannot cook one pan or casserole of food, the dish can be made worse because of too many cooks. To avoid a saturation of salt, hot pepper, oil, tomatoes, onions, water and other ingredients, it would be advantageous to allow one cook to focus on preparing the entrée. Too many suggestions from so many different cooks may ruin the entire meal.

That is why the principle protocols must be followed in order to settle on a good tentative solution in the case of separation, divorce an reconciliation inside the marriage. One Congolese proverb says: "Tentative is not always a synonym of succeeding but we, human being must always try." This was also an encouragement for me Elie to overcome the marriage difficulties in my life.

Seen here with colleagues, Elie's extensive work with the Peace Corps also draws him to D.C.

Chapter 3
FOUR TYPES OF MARRIAGE IN THE DEMOCRATIC REPUBLIC OF CONGO

What are the four types of marriage, weddings and dating in the DRC?

Preferential Marriage

In the Democratic of Congo in particular and in Africa in general, marriage is accepted as a social contract and an affectionate relationship between the two spouses. As long as the intimacy, love, confidence, trust, and patience grow between the two lovers, they have a moral obligation to inform their partners on both side, the groom, and the bride first and then the extended family later. This type of marriage is called "Preferential marriage."

However, it takes time, even years of negations for relatives on both sides to meet, discuss and talk about issues before and after the marriage. Each one of the four (4) types of the marriage may have more wedding ceremonies: traditional, civil, and religious. But all depends on the structure and the social life of the families. The groom's family suffers the most financially because they have to pay a lot of money to the bride's family for raising their daughter. For example, they may provide items such as money, clothes, food, live animals, a traditional palm tree, or a sugar tree, wine, jewelry, lamps, lingerie, shoes, coffee, tea, etc.

Arranged Marriage

Before the 1990's, this type of marriage was very popular among the families in the DRC. To be very honest with you my readers, I am one of those who was a victim of this type of marriage. My fiancée's parents and my parents had months of negotiations that focused on the moral obligations on both sides.

The arranged marriage today, according to the opinion or verbal statistics, works only ten percent of the time. Ninety percent of the arranged marriages break up and end up in divorce before or after having children. There tends to be so much incompatibility between these spouses. The misunderstanding, the conditional love, the lack of agreement and other conflicts make the relationship so difficult for the marriage partners to settle down and live together. Often, the two families will feud back and forth to assuage conflicts. For this type of arranged marriage, many disagreements will occur during their marriage.

For example, cheating, or finding a concubine, which we call "Spare Tire or Second Office," often ends these relationships.

Interest (Profitable) Marriage

Love is not the center key between the two spouses, because all it is about is making profit by both parties. It is clearly and simply scarifying the future wife and husband to the detriment of the parents' families. While no trace of intimacy exists between the two spouses, the parents or families of both sides meet on their own to discuss and decide on the distribution and beneficiaries of the family wealth. In one way it is seen more like a corruption.

For example 1: Since there are too many women who cannot find men to marry them, the bride's family will corrupt the groom's family with a couple of cows and goats so that their son marries their daughter.

Example 2: The bride's family may buy a house or some land which includes a built house, and influences the groom's family so that their son falls in love with the girl in the bride's family.

Since there is not true love, this may result in spouses cheating or finding a secret lover called "Spare Tire or Second Office."

Forced (Obliged) Marriage

Elie B. Mbumina

Traditionally, the forced (obliged) marriage occurs when two cousins—a boy and girl—from the paternal side will be forced to become husband and wife. The literal translation of this marriage procedure is called "returning the blood in the same family." This means you are not going anywhere to find a husband or a wife. You are locked up in the middle of nowhere else and in the middle of nothing else. You will be yelling, screaming and crying like a little baby. We don't care because you are locked up and sealed in the box, meaning you both spouses can't be off the hook nor off the chains, cheating or not. That's all, period!

It is very challenging putting young people in a very difficult position like this. It hurts so bad for the young couple. Many see it as an incestuous union. At these times, many young people truly become the scapegoats. Like or not, there is constant revolt to this marriage.

The reason why these families follow this tradition is because they need and want to conserve their family's wealth and avoid joining with other families. But realistically, this doesn't make sense. The good news is that this type of marriage is declining. progressively. Thank you, God!

In the Democratic Republic of Congo (DRC) the role of the family and friendship ties are so strong; in fact, the moral obligations are well reinforced and respected by all.

People believe in sharing some basic, necessary values and amenities, such as food, money, and shelter. Also, they have a very good sense of solidarity, hospitality, kindness, generosity, and goodness. Also, they understand that raising children is everyone's responsibility. They tend to believe in this proverb: "It takes the entire village to raise a child." This simply means that when a child is born, that child belongs to everybody and no child can be left behind.

For example, in these very hard, harsh and difficult moments of the COVID-19 and during the Pandemic, distant relatives or extended family members or people from the surrounding cities and locations may expect friends, neighbors, families to host and feed them at no costs regardless of the outcome of the hardship this provision might cause them. In other words, helping others is a moral obligation and a sign of blessings.

These traditions, stereotypes and customs are practically reinforced because in the DRC, people have common bonds to serve instead of always being served all the time.

We certainly applaud President John F. Kennedy, in the United States who inspired children and adults during his inaugural address on January 20, 1961 when he exhorted all people to contribute to the public good. Kennedy said, "Ask not what your country can do for you, but ask what you can do for your country." During the conclusion of this speech, Kennedy launched the organization called the Peace Corps where men and woman could help others in need.

People tend to place their personal interest as a priority and later be united with a good organization where they can serve, no matter what difficult challenges or obstacles might deter them.

The less fortunate people, such as those who have handicaps, those who are orphans, or widows often receive support from others who have more to share with them. Also, the practice of individualism is often banned because people like to work together as a team in many cases. What a solidarity!

This helps ease tension, lowers high blood pressure, which can be a pain in the butt. This mechanism is sometimes altered because of the financial hardship, changes of Mother Nature, social life, sickness, moving to a different village or town, but the family ties in the community and society stay solid.

Washington also came to Elie in 2008 when he attended the Obama/Biden campaign rally. Elie was near the rostrum.

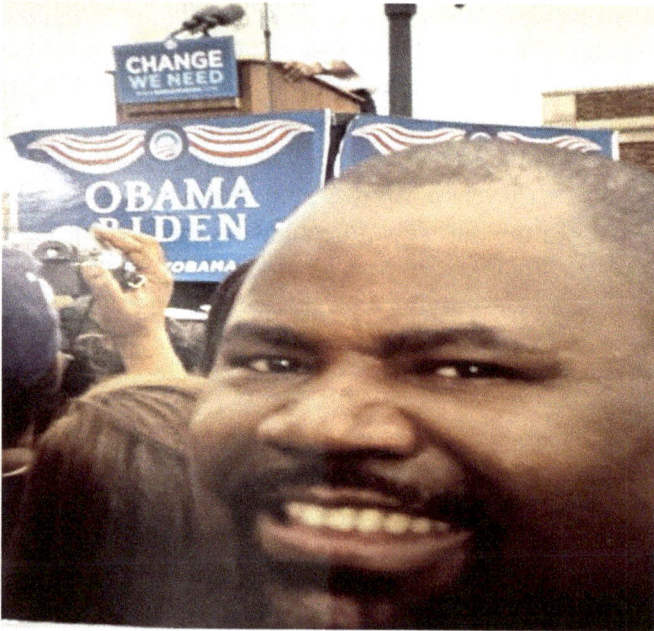

CHAPTER 4
SEXUALITY, PREGNANCY, PROSTITUTION, DIVORCE, AND ABORTION IN THE DEMOCRATIC REPUBLIC OF CONGO

The typical lifestyle including the standard of living in the DRC are variant from one city to another or from one territory to another. It all depends on individual background, childhood education and the environment where one lives from birth to adolescence commonly called teenagers.

Sexuality

Many decades ago, sexuality was considered and viewed as a nice surprise during the first day or night only after getting married. Most women and men used to get married while being a virgin state (status). No sexual activities were allowed during the teenage, adolescent, even the adult stage, or during girlhood, even during boyhood or between fiancées.

In most cases, the sexual activities after marriage took place under the supervision of one of the aunts on the father's side of the family during the wedding night. It was the aunt's responsibility to teach, train and coach the new couple on how to perform sex on low, medium or high gear in the marriage bed. She also taught them the different positions as such as missionary position meaning men on top and woman under, training them on the different angles and directions: 30 degrees, 60 degrees, 90 degrees, 180 degrees, etc. . . . for the positions of the legs as well as balancing with the different movements and dances to the left, to the right, to the south, to the north and then hitting hand like a man. Oral sex was less encouraged during

Elie B. Mbumina

sexual relations nor after sexual intimacy.

However, this is one of the most frequently asked questions people are asking me today:

Q. Elie, why did a young, healthy man like you grow up without a sex life and why were you still a virgin at twenty-five years old?

A. Well, personally, I have few convincing reasons: I was born in a Christian family, and I was spiritually nurtured at the hands of the missionaries from Sweden who came to the Republic Democratic of Congo (DRC). Since 1881, over 100 years ago, my parents—Madam Helene Nzuzi and Mr. Elie Mbumina—and the missionaries raised me with a such a disciplined practice of obedience to the Word of God and with the fear of God over my sins. I even developed in myself the shyness for having a simple conversation with girls. I used to think that a good conversation with a girl could lead to sexual intercourse or sexual favors. That kind of mentality made me refrain from talking to the young girls or having relationships with them.

Pregnancy

Another fear during my adolescence age was impregnating a girl. During that time, we did not know any methods proved by the medicine or scientists to prevent pregnancies. Any pregnancy outside the marriage was considered as a real catastrophe for the two partners, the families, communities and societies. In most cases like this one, the young man was coerced to marry the girl like her or not. His school career was in jeopardy as well.

In addition, the parents and the large family of the young man who impregnated the young girl were all forced to pay an exorbitant of money, animals and goods to the parents and family of the young girl. This kind of compensation was set up to ease the anger and escalated tension between the two large families and their friends. However, one proverb was always reinforced: "Raise your own baby!"

What a punishment—moral torture and disastrous

60

consequences—impregnating a young girl in our adolescence times!

Many elders would scare us by telling us that if anyone impregnates a girl, instead of cutting off the young man's private part, they will massage the young man's phallus with hot pepper and then administer corporal punishment by beating him with a stick. Following this, the young man would be tied with cords followed by the ritual of pushing his head to the ground and letting him use his mouth and tongue to kiss the soil very hard and swear by saying, "I will not do it again!"

Prostitution

In my original country, back years ago, prostitution was almost nonexistent due to the families' backgrounds and cultural education. It truly was a shameful profession. Another change that took place is that polygamy was authorized in the communities and society.

However, polyandria, a woman having a plurality of husbands at the same time, was not officially accepted. While many men were still getting married to multiple women at the same time, the women were not allowed to do the same. All these women may live in one single house with several bedrooms, or they may live separately from each other. If they all live in one house or separately, the man will have the obligation to make daily and weekly tours to sexually and morally satisfy each one of his wives.

For example: If a man has three wives, he must spend two nights a week with each woman. The seventh night of the week is for the man to recharge his battery, meaning to rest and recuperate his lost energy from the sexual activities.

The man will do whatever he can within his ability to take care his wives and children. However, with his limited income, it is always impossible for him to financially provide for all the wives. This is why his women must work very hard in agriculture and crops to sell their agricultural products and support their children and themselves and also support their husband in many cases.

For example: Each woman must cook a dish to put on the table. The leftovers from each meal will be collected and saved or will be given to the children.

On special occasions such as Holiday Christmas seasons and other holidays, the husband and all his wives and children with some invited friends will have lunch or dinner together. The food is served with traditional alcohol beverages for the adults and with various choices, such as Palm Tree Wine or Sugar Cane Wine.

However, in America, polygamy and polyandria are prohibited, except those who practice them in hiding or in secret as "secret lovers."

Abortion

Historically, abortion was and still is a major problem among women. The lack of using birth control methods has crested a major rise in unwanted pregnancies among fertile people who are sexually active. Churches and state government agree on the abolition of abortion. However, the biggest unresolved question is how can the states make this tough rule work?

The biggest concern on the abortion laws in the Democratic Republic of Congo (DRC) is that this careless government does not provide decent jobs with a working wage; nor do they provide minimum wage to those who are employed in any sectors. Many people have been sacrificed, neglected and disgraced by their own DRC government. They barely make one to two dollars a day. What a starvation! What a misery! What a disgrace!

Parents cannot put food on the table. The elders find it difficult to control young women on the streets who are selling their bodies just to buy food, clothes and shelter. It is not only sad, but also very disgusting watching the seven-year-old girls and older women selling their bodies on the streets to take care of themselves and their family members. In cases like this, parents have no control over their little girls because they, too, are powerless, unable to provide for their families, yet corrupted by the food their young relatives bring to the table.

The other problems which encourage prostitution among the young girls, adults and even married women are that parents are unable to send their children to school because they cannot afford to pay tuition and fees for their children to go to school. Parents cannot afford to buy school supplies due to the lack of incomes, jobs, and courage.

In order for the girls in the Democratic Republic of Congo (DRC) to pass their courses, they have two options. If they cannot find the money to pay the teachers, the other option is to sell their bodies to the instructors. The young women have no choice, because many of them are involved with involuntary sex. Can you believe that the richest country in the world, The Democratic Republic of Congo (DRC), teeming with natural resources, minerals, gold, diamonds, cobalt for the fabrication of batteries, cars, iPhones, Android phones, manganese, copper, phosphate, zinc, aluminum, uranium, oil. Wood, coal, and coffee has such a challenge to educate young people? The Democratic Republic of Congo possesses many natural resources found in the entire world, but this country needs to find a way to provide education for its children. So many concerns impact the DRC, such as massacres, genocide, rapes, ungainly occupations, and balkanization (15 million plus dead) since the 1990's. The United Nations USA World Health Organization, MONESCO, World Bank, Multi-Nationals, etc. are all very aware of this tragic situation in the DRC.

So, what really needs to be done to curtail this immoral, heinous, and horrible prostitution in the DRC? All top official government officials are paid $15,000 per month, but common citizens earn only $30 to $50 per month. The government needs to make the safety and provision of its citizens a major priority. The new DRC government must be imminent in order to resolve the prostitution issue and other difficult problems the population is facing. Hope, faith prayers, courage, perseverance, commitment, and determination are in fact needed to overcome these obstacles when are heavily demoralizing and disgracing the people of the DRC.

I personally and frankly believe that these polarizing

situations of sexuality, pregnancy, prostitution, divorce, and abortion can and will be resolved by having a good conscience in electing people or officials who are well-educated, polished, and shaped to do the work that needs to be done in the DRC.

I certainly believe in what former United States President John F. Kennedy said in his inaugural speech to the nation: "Ask not what your country can do for you, but ask what you can do for your country." The United States of America is a great country with great values even though they still have some problems. With the help, education, and progress from the industrialized countries, the DRC government must learn valuable lessons to do the right things for its population and move forward into the future.

As a professor at North Carolina State University in Greensboro, Elie worked along with Dr. Durham to organize a trip to Brazil in 2006. Above, he stands a group students before the famous statue of Christ the Redeemer. Below, Elie stands alone before the statue.

Elie B. Mbumina

CHAPTER 5
MY FIRST SIN WITH A WOMAN
WHEN I WAS A VIRGIN AT
THIRTY YEARS OLD

Wow! What an unbelievable experience with a mix of feelings! Positive, negative, confusing, uncertain, excited, so many emotions.

I believe that a human being can easily forget a lot of memories. He or she goes through his or her life, but it is close to impossible to forget the first date or the first intercourse between two friends of the opposite sex who have been involved in sexual activities. I certainly think that when two friends of the opposite sex meet regularly or frequently and they become good close friends or associates, it will be almost impossible down the road to abstain from the sexual activities or intercourse. History may be good or bad; the past experience for each of us on earth may be pleasant or unkind, but we will never change our history. We can change our own behavior and habits according to our past, present, and our future projection and anticipation. Some events of our lives are locked away in our long-term memories, and our sexual encounters hold fast to our brain waves whether we think we made a mistake or if we selected the best partner we could ever choose.

Most importantly, we people are better off to learn by drawing a good clear lesson from our mistakes made in the past. Nobody is perfect except our Heavenly Father, the Creator of the heaven, earth, and the whole universe with His son Jesus Christ.

I know and understand that it takes exceptional courage to talk about sexual sins like fornication and adultery. Most of us are afraid and discouraged to talk about temptation and our participation in it, unless making some confession at church or to a pastor in some instances. Nobody wants to be humiliated or to be bullied or mocked because of his or her sins. For example, is it acceptable to have sex without being married as long as you

66

don't get caught? Really? Who is trying to fool whom here? In many churches, communities, and societies, people don't want to talk about this sex subject because many single church members are sexually active. We also allow our teenagers to engage in sexual acts with their girlfriends and boyfriends in the house, on the couch, in the woods, in the pool, at dances and parties, while camping, or on school trips.

I still remember when I did it with my girlfriend for the first time when I was twenty-five years old. My girlfriend and I went on a date that night. After coming back from the date and restaurant, we decided to have a couple of drinks, meaning a couple of beers, but no cigarettes because we were not smokers. This entire evening episode happened in my apartment. Suddenly, she started to touch me, and I started to touch her back. By that moment, I felt a big change that affected my entire body, but I was afraid and shaky about what was about to happen because I was a virgin, and I did not know how to do it right.

Later on that night, we both were playing and laughing, and the alcohol really started to work on both of us. I said to her, "Ooh lala, Madam!" Then we started to kiss each other. Then I had the courage to call her with the words "Madam," "My Babe," "My Lady!" I told her that I was still a virgin. Here is the short conversation we had at that very special moment while I was experiencing a high-speed erection from my side.

She said, "Oh my gosh! I feel terrible! And you made me orgasm!"

We had a conversation while touching and kissing each other:

Question: "Madam."
Answer: "Yes."
Question: "May I tell you something?"
Answer: "Yes. Go ahead, My Love."
Question: "Please, do not laugh at me. Can I trust you?"
Answer: "Oh no! I won't laugh at you, My Love."
Question: "I am a virgin. . . Did you hear me?"
Answer: "What? Are you serious!? At your age, you are still a virgin? How old are you now?"

Elie B. Mbumina

Question: "I am twenty-five years old. Can you please teach me?"

Answer: "Okay, don't worry. I will teach you and train you how to have good sex!"

Question: "May I ask your permission to kiss your breast, neck, hips, etc...?"

Answer: "Permission! Okay. You get so hard, and I feel it. But take it easy. Take all your clothes off and I will do the same."

Question: "Oh, Madam. You are so beautiful! You are very nice, attractive and I love you so much!"

Answer: "Thank you. You are very kind, nice and very attractive too. You are doing very well. I was very surprised and fell in love with you when you said the word permission."

Question: "Yes, Madam. It is my obligation to ask your permission first."

Answer: "Oh my love. You are the first man in all my life who chose to ask me nicely for permission to have sex and most importantly to teach you how to do it, where to kiss in order to turn a woman on and heat this up."

Question: "Thank you very much for teaching me everything, including all different kinds of tongue and sexual positions to make sex very interesting."

Answer: "You are very welcome and I want to tell you that you did such a wonderful job by making me cry from sexual pleasure."

Question: "Oh, thank you again, Madame! I will never forget this wonderful sex experience with you my first woman. How do you think I did?"

Answer: "Oh, you did excellent, and I have a very good surprise news for you. You graduate with honors for sex. Please keep this up. Keep up this excellent job!"

After that pleasure that night, I felt so good. On the one hand, I felt so excited, but I felt so inexperienced on the other hand. The very positive thing for me was that I learned the sexual life at twenty-five years old, and it was so good and neat. I felt soooooooooooo goooooooooooood!"

But the negative thing was that I committed fornication. It

was telling my conscience that I have to confess at church one day and I did. I started telling myself: "What hope, faith, and courage I had." Feeling good in one way, but feeling guilty in another way for participating in a lovely experience that could also be considered sinful. This can be challenging because it can keep me up and down on a roller coaster ride. The joy can lift me up, but the guilt can hijack me, hunt me down for a while and push me into repentance and confession.

In the French language, we always say, "*C'est la vie.*" This means, "That is life." Life does go on. I cannot just stand still and mark time. This new experience has moved me forward. Sometimes people walk on the sleeper or wait roads. We can easily fall down and stand up again quickly and continue until we get to our final destination, reaching for our objectives.

What went wrong? After the assessment and the evaluation of this romantic night, I found out that we both were ready to have a good sex and in the meantime, the consumption of alcohol indeed contributed as a catalyst, an enzyme and accelerator to fire up, hit up and start up my engine! Her orgasm was like a space shuttle going to the moon!

What happened? Frankly, before our sexual activities that night, I did not know that sweet, kind and lovely words accompanied with physical touch, kisses, rubs all over a woman's body would quickly turn her on and make her moist down there. The moisture flowed from the bottom to the lovely bean, the clitoris, and the breast nipples stood at attention. A woman is a perfectly lovely creation of God! I will no longer feel guilty about celebrating His creation.

Why so crazy?

To be honest, that first great, awesome and incomparable sexual pleasure made me scream in the unknown tongue like crazy. I felt like I was in the clouds. I love that great, hot, juicy stuff! Yes! I love it! AND LICKING THE VERY NICE ATTRACTIVE RED BEAN IN THE MIDDLE! OoooHHH LAAAALLAAAAAAA! What great, attractive perfume down there! OOh la la! Everything was excellent, sweet and a great salted taste.

In 2000, Elie was able to visit Myrtle Beach with friends.

Chapter 6
CONCLUSION

I would like to conclude my storytelling by asking a couple of questions in a nice way:

1. Have you already heard about somebody or someone being perfect in this entire world?

2. Who has never sinned on this planet?

3. Besides God and Jesus, is there anyone who can throw a rock at me for being an imperfect sinner because he or she is without sin?

4. Have you been courageous to do your confession or repentance?

5. What valuable lesson did you learn from God during your life and during my story?

Thank you kindly.

May God continue to bless all of us, forgive our sins through our confessions and our repentance. Most importantly, we have to love these irreplaceable sweethearts! OOOhhhlaaalaaa! Lovely women!

Indeed, my first sin during a date with a woman when I still was a virgin at twenty-five years of age taught me a good, valuable lesson in my life. Learning from scratch in the middle of nothing and nowhere can be very challenging to anyone. Frustration, anxiety, pain, happiness, encouragement, joy, etc. can occur during those special positive or negative moments of our learnings. Sometimes we get the feeling to keep up with it or abandon it depending upon the outcome that we experience from them. I know for sure that I am not a perfect man; only GOD is. But I have the courage, commitment, determination, perseverance, hope, and faith to do the right thing with the GRACE OF GOD. We really, truly must respect our women because they are our special, lovely wives, our lovely moms who

71

Elie B. Mbumina

give birth to us, and they are awesome and excellent companions in our lives. They are just ooohhhlalala romantic, unique creatures. They make a lot of mistakes in their lives just like men, but we have to work this out together.

Marriage Song in the Congo
"The Love We Share"

When two people love each other
They become lovers heart-to-heart,
Yes, you eat my heart and I eat yours.
Love, Love, Love, baby—babe—be'be'

Songs for SCOUT and for JEUNIPRO (Protestant) International Youth

1. "How Proud You are Congolese Youth!"
Congolese International Youth,
How Proud you are!

> *In Kikongo Language:*
> *Bana Congo mu mikuma,*
> *!Yolele du monde yo! . . .*

2. "We Will Meet Again Because It's Just a Bye"
In French/English Language

> *Pour ceux qui nous quittent sans Espoir . . .*
> *For those who are leaving us without hope to meet again . . .*
> *Ce n'est qu'un Au Revoir mes chers, . . .*
> *It is just a Good Bye, my dears, . . .*
> *Oui—Oui nous—reverrons mes chers*
> *Yes—Yes we will see and meet again my dears.*
> *Ce n' est qu'um Au Revoir—It is just a Good Bye.*

Proverbs

1. Do not be greedy, but share with others to become full birth.

2. Humility, respect, and obedience always pay off (are

72

worthy).

3.The first courageous people in the morning are those who always get the fresh, clean drinking water. But the lazy ones are always those who drink the dirty water.

4.Nothing is greater than the love that we all share.

5.Help yourself first before the skies will; before depending on someone else.

6.Take time to decide on your future wife/husband because it is not a flea market where all good produce/products will be gone in only a few days.

7.Pick/select your fiance' by his/her true heart instead of his/her beauty because he/she may be having sex with multiple partners.

Part 3

How, Why, and to What Extent American Peace Corps Professors and Missionaries Groomed, Shaped, Polished, Blessed and Loved Me By Shaping My Life Through Education

Elie B. Mbumina, Ph.D., Professor, Interpreter, Translator, Writer, Missionary, and World Traveler

Introduction

Dear Readers, Colleagues, Educators, Professors, Faculty members, Scholars and Parents!

As written in my two previous books, I would like to express once more my sincere gratitude to all of you and to my family members for reading this book. I am grateful for your comments, your suggestions, and your money to buy this book. It is customary for me to express that I am always very appreciative for your support.

Once again, I would like to nail this up by informing you that your contributions, donations, or tokens will be dedicated in service to assisting the Christian Evangelical and Missionary Churches founded in 1881. Also, just keep in mind that a portion of the proceeds will be used in planting church buildings in various locations for the purposes of worship, Sunday School classes, Bible studies, and or assisting special-needs children, widows, and handicapped persons. Also, an additional portion of these funds will be donated to our American Peace Corps organization.

My Incredible Story

I would like to announce that the invitation has been extended to any American or Canadian financial advisers to join me in coordinating the operational budgets and work once the monetary donations and gifts start to roll in.

For all your monetary contributions to smoothly enhance these Evangelical Christian and Missionary operations, please refer to the information below. Your hearty financial assistance will be greatly appreciated. They will provide a great deal of support through monetary donations to cover the high cost of publishing this text.

Also, for your heads up, for your information and excitement, please be informed or reminded that there are three books on the market at Amazon that will not only give you the new insights of very important missing information for life, but also these three books will bring you a lot of excitement and happiness, joy, laughter, entertainment, inspiration and knowledge. May God bless all of the readers, bless Amazon and the owners—Madam and Mr. Jeff Bezos—and bless the United States of America.

Here are the lovely and exciting three recommended books all combined in one block for your pleasure and enjoyment.

Chapter 1

I was born in the Democratic Republic of Congo, Africa, and I spent my childhood with my parents, Mr. Elie Mbumina and Mrs. Helen Nzuzi. I have seven siblings—two brothers and five sisters—all born in the Democratic Republic of Congo (DRC), located in the center of Africa.

What then makes my family unique, special, popular loved, and attractive to virtually all who meet them? The answer is quite simple:

First of all, both of my parents, Papa Elie Mbumina and Mama Helene Nzuzi were born in the DRC in the 1930s. Unfortunately, during their early childhood, my Papa lost his mother, and my Mama lost both of her parents.

Mama Helene Nzuzi is a twin, and her identical twin sister is named Albertine Nsimba. Please be informed that in my state of Bas-Congo in the Democratic Republic of Congo, twins carry very significant names. It doesn't matter whether the twins are boys or girls, the oldest is named Nzuzi, and the youngest is named Nsimba.

What caused the drama to both of my beautiful, pretty, and smart twin mothers? And what has happened to my special Dad? Although both twins were indescribably geniuses, nobody could afford to provide for their schooling. Therefore, the word about their lack of financial backing quickly spread all the way to the Swedish Missionary Schools in Sundi-Lutete. From there, the missionaries decided to adopt the oldest twin named Helene Nzuzi, who is my mother. The youngest twin, Albertine Nsimba, could not be adopted because she was taking care of the youngest sibling Antoinette Nlandu.

In the 1950s, both my parents were grateful and lucky of being educated at Swedish Evangelical Missionary School (EEMM-SMF) in Sundi-Lutete. In the entire school, my mother Helen Nzuzi and Rebecca Mpola were the only two female students. Mrs. Helene Nzuzi (my mom) and Mrs. Rebecca Mpola were the only scholars in the entire missionary school. The missionaries gave tremendously, financially, mentally, and materially to support the only two female students in the entire school. Also, my mother became a babysitter for Swedish missionaries and later for the other missionaries from Scandinavia, Belgium, England, Canada, the United States, and the American Peace Corps followed and added more schools with different Christian church denominations, such as Church of Christ, Baptist, Presbyterian, Lutheran, Pentecostal, and Methodist.

After graduation, my parents started their teaching careers in education as instructors. Unfortunately, my father ascended to heaven about twelve years ago. However, my mom has been teaching more than seventy years. She cannot retire from her teaching job because the Congolese government stole all the teachers' retirement funds. What a disgrace! Now my mother just continues to teach for her livelihood without the possibility of retirement.

It is so bad and sad to have a criminally corrupt, toxic political system in the Democratic Republic of Congolese! Please keep in mind that all teachers who worked so hard in the Congolese school system since the 1950s until the present have never been paid even one dime for their retirement funds. The worst is that many of them died due to the stress, anxiety, high blood pressure, and suicide attempts from working sixty to seventy years, without getting any benefits from their retirements. What a horrible, terrible disgrace for them! They also suffer from malnutrition, exhaustion, and lack of clothing.

In the DRC, I spent over ninety percent of my entire life there in the Christian boarding schools. My mother taught me in first grade, and my father taught me in second grade on the elementary school level. Both of my parents were tough, severe, and strict on disciplinary actions. They used the mix of corporal and vocal disciplinary methods for our education. I remember that my mother used to tell me, "Elie, never call me Mom in the classroom, but call me Madam Teacher Helene."

Elie B. Mbumina

Their special teaching pedagogical methodology and psychology was very systematic, a combination of all educational methodologies which send clear messages and signals to all students by reminding all of us that the teachers are not only serious about us, but they are focused also on different future challenges for the learning process. They wanted to give us a solid foundation to make us the best that we could be. The strong motto was "Enter to learn and depart to serve." We know for sure that receiving knowledge, money, or service is good, but giving, sharing or providing a service to people is always better.

Chapter 2

At elementary school in Sundi-Kimbonga, Democratic Republic of the Congo, students had to study very hard to avoid repeating the school year. This school education system was set up early in the Nineteenth Century by the ex-colonial country Belgium and used before and after the independence on June 30, 1960.

During the 2012 visit of Pope John Paul, DRC women work on the DEC/SMF plantation.

From the third grade to the sixth grade, I moved to a different boarding school of Sundi- Mamba, Democratic Republic of the Congo. The only time I was visited my family was on weekends. During that brief family visit, I helped my parents with household chores, agricultural projects, plantation work, and especially fishing work. At night, we would sit down around the storyteller to listen to those fabulous stories, proverbs, tales, and learn by drawing valuable lessons from them. Also, we used to hold hands together and sing different songs in a merry-go-round fashion. We had fun together during my home visits, but the disciplinary actions continued, and curfew was still reinforced every night at 8:30 P.M., and everyone had to be in bed by 9:00 P.M., without any exceptions. Corporate punishment was often reinforced as well. The moral and civic education level started at a very early age. Learning how to do things correctly was crucial. We, students had to attend church services every week and were required to pass the religion class to move to the next level.

After receiving my certification at the end of the sixth grade, I moved to a different school in Kinkenge, Democratic Republic of Congo, for my seventh and eighth grade called "Orientation Cycle," because the education system in DRC requires students to chose their future major related to their future job assignment before taking the state exam at the end of the eighth grade.

I became heavily involved in the choir, in soccer tournaments, in scout meetings and the dancing team. Even though I was having a lot of fun in this school, I had to make sure I was doing my schoolwork properly, efficiently and in a timely fashion because it seriously was no joke.

Due to the school load, materials, discipline, and the time constraints, I was going back at home only three times a year: Christmas, Easter, and at the end of the year in July. I remember watching my very first movie at the age of fifteen. It was a Swedish movie shown by the Swedish missionaries at school. The movie was called "Sweden in Winter." The film portrayed how the Swedish parents and their children loved the snow. During a heavy snowstorm, the children scooped up big bowls of snow under their snow tents. The children were playing in the snow, hitting one another with balls of ice and eating the snow like ice cream. The snow looked so cold, but oh so pretty. What an experience seeing a snow for the first time during my first movie!

At the end of the eighth grade, after successfully passing my state exam, I was sent to Sona-Bata for my ninth through twelfth grade of High School called "Humanity-Secondaire." It was very interesting because we were taught by professors from different organizations and church denominations: American

Peace Corps; Canadian missionaries; Dutch-Belgian missionaries; Egyptian professors; and Congolese professors.

In the DRC, there are about forty percent Catholic believers, fifty percent Protestant believers and ten percent of other religions. However, all denominations work together as a team. Student exchange is very common between Catholic and Protestant schools. The liturgical exchange between pastors and choir members is tolerant between different church denominations.

The moral dimensions remain somewhat influenced or disconnected inside the school systems due to many factors, such as women's emancipation, equality between men and women, the conflict of inferiority-complexity between genders, human rights, freedom of speech, equal opportunities, role of the activist, the role of the artist, and the like.

By comparing the current Congolese society with that of the 1960s, many rules have changed in schools, communities and societies.

In addition, the comparison and the contrast that I would like to make between the American Peace Corps and the Missionaries regarding the exceptional education, the care and the encouragement that I received from both sides by grooming me, shaping me, polishing me, blessing me, equipping me, and loving me is quite easy to understand:

The American Peace Corps, on one hand, was founded in the 1960s by our great and famous President John F. Kennedy, and were sent almost around the world. When they were sent to my original country, the Democratic Republic of Congo (DRC), they quickly became very well-known for their noble actions, education, services for accomplishing their goals and objectives in a timely fashion. What is more, they earned a reputation for saving lives as well. Wow! What a great privilege and opportunity for me to benefit from their fantastic work and services! I am so grateful, and thankful, and very proud of all of these services. The American Peace Corps, with its diversity of qualifications, having worked in schools, hospitals, maternity wards, farms, mines, technology, logistics, etc.

Elie B. Mbumina

Before coming to America to complete my education, I was educated at schools in the DRC by some of the greatest professors from the American Peace Corps"

Professor Tina Thuermer for English; Professor Martha Brown for Math and Physics; Professor Daniel Tamulonis for English; Professor Rob Willis for Biology and Chemistry; Professor Jim Freeman for Math; and Professor Amy Mellencamp for English. Therefore, my message is that these wonderful, awesome, and great professors of all times made me and so many other students the best products or scholars that we can be, and we remain exceptional today. They positively impacted our lives and our futures. We all became a great family. Most of us now have a better life, better jobs, and we have traveled around the world to impact others.

Thank you, God that I did not take things for granted. Thank you again to all of our professors! America how great you are! May God bless you. God bless America! The American and Canadian and European missionaries, mostly from Sweden (Scandinavia) and the Catholic priests from Belgium, Netherland (Holland), England and Italy, on the other hand, started coming to the Democratic Republic of Congo (DRC) in the 1890s.

The missionaries, with their incomparable mission, vision and legacy, they equip me along with the other ordinary people with the Bible study, religion study, and the story of health matters. Their role and duty were similar in one way to those of the American Peace Corps—to teach different subjects in school as well. Missionaries planed more Christian church buildings in order to preach the gospel, to assist and serve better as well as to fulfill the essential needs for the vulnerable and the disabled— the handicapped children with chronic illnesses, physical limitations and assisting desperate orphans and widows as well.

Frankly, I was well-equipped as a learner through a solid formative, secondary, and college education, and a complete immersion in a solid spiritual education. Even though the missionaries brought in the DRC, and in many parts of the world, there are many diverse Christian church denominations, they always checked and verified that they reconnected by forming a true solid partnership between the Congolese, the American, the Canadian, Swedish, British, Dutch, Italian, and many other church affiliations. All of the Christian denominations were expected to work together as a team for their noble work, mission and vision. Their ultimate goal was always to connect with hope, faith, and love.

The most Christian Church denominations in the Democratic Republic of the Congo are the Church of Christ, the Baptist Church, the Pentecostal Church, the Methodist Church, the Arme'e du Salut Church, the Presbyterian Church, the Way Church, the Bramam Church, the Kimbanquist Church, and the Catholic Church. The good news about the church variety is that the Catholic Church and all other Protestant churches work together as a team.

Finally, I am not perfect, but I am very grateful and blessed to be groomed, shaped polished, equipped, and loaded with the Word of God, effective school education through the missionaries, the American Peace Corps professors, and other instructors and experiences. May God bless them all!

Elie and fellow travelers visited Sweden in 2011, staying in the home of Mr. Yngve, pictured on the left.

Chapter 3

Becoming groomed, shaped, polished, blessed, and unconditionally loved by the American Peace Corps, professors, and missionaries from the United States of America, Canada, and Europe gave all of us the training and confident professionalism to proceed from our training ground into leading others.

In July of 2023, I was coordinating the visit of our school alumni from our High School of Sona-Bata in Zaire, DRC (Democratic Republic of Congo) who were visiting the American Peace Corps professors and staff members in Washington, DC. I also served as a bridge by connecting our school alumni, teachers, professors, and staff to the American Peace Corps professors in the United States of America and around the world. Our mission was to thank them for the wonderful work they did in the DRC. What great moments and life's souvenirs we all had and shared together! Oo la la!

We all keep those great moments bursting in our hearts. For example, our fellow Americans are still keeping those highlights of the fight between Muhammad Ali and George Foreman in Kinshasa, Zaire (DRC) on October 30, 1974. When the "Rumble in the Jungle" aired on television on that day, as many as one billion people watched the fight worldwide.

The close relationship that I had with the American Peace Corps professors and missionaries, the Swedish professors, and the missionaries, including the Belgian, French, and Italian professors and priests indeed helped me to materialize my sweet dream.

I knew I had to face many challenges head through my school education and prior to my long trip to the United States of America for the main goal of completing my education in America.

My Incredible Story

Sometimes I was facing a great deal of uncertainty, questions for the future of my life, but I was focused, mentally prepared with courage, full of hope, faith, prayer, commitment, dedication, determination, and perseverance.

By believing and trusting God and having confidence in myself, I was able to push forward and accomplish extraordinary things. By following the rules and regulations of my school, and most importantly, obeying my wonderful professors to study conscientiously and following the school leaders' instructions, I found myself ending up on top of all my homework assignments and other classwork. Therefore, my application of the procedures and my conduct was always above expectation. What a successful school life! "Enter to Learn, Depart to Serve." While this was the motto of Winston-Salem State University, this adage also applied to my academic accomplishment during my tenure in the American Peace Corps.

Finally, coming from the Democratic Republic of Congo, formerly called Zaire, becoming well-educated there from my parents and my American Peace Corps professors and missionaries, Canadian professors, and missionaries from Europe, I definitely became groomed, shaped, polished, blessed, loved and guess what? I also became a center of attraction, a center of gravity, and a center of interest by the community, the society and across the world through my jobs, careers and experiences. May God bless my family, my professors, missionaries, and the United States of America, Canada and Europe.

For Donations or Contributions, Readers may contact the author at PO Box 1235, Greensboro, NC 27402 or via mbuminae@aol.com, elie.contactchoir@gmail.com, or contact@evangelicalchoirandservices.com, or by calling (336) 988-0989 or (336) 202-6794

www.ingramcontent.com/pod-product-compliance
Lightning Source LLC
Chambersburg PA
CBHW060055100426
42742CB00014B/2849